D1173678

The Law of Action:

Master Key to the Universe We *Actually* Live In

THEO E.J. WILSON

ISBN: 0578189208
ISBN-13: 978-0-578-18920-8

DEDICATION

To those with the intellectual honesty and moral courage to follow the evidence wherever it leads them. To those whose compassion and love make evident the oneness obscured by the illusion of separateness. To those who understand that nothing exists but the truth, and have dedicated their lives to its expedient revelation.

CONTENTS

ACKNOWLEDGMENTS

I'd like to thank my parents whose example is a constant reminder of the excellence in ordinary people. Thank you to my team for holding me accountable as much as they hold me upon their shoulders. Thank you to my community whose culture and energy is the foundational bedrock of my intellectual life. Thank you to the fans and followers whose love I seek to reward with service.

Foreword:

Imagine if you will, a world where truth...tangible, actionable, wrap-your-arms-around it truth, is at such a premium that the mere mention of it could send grown men and women into frenzied tears of joy, and others into outrageous fear and loathing. Some warned us of this world. People like George Orwell, Franz Fanon, and that famous unknown philosopher who wrote "In a time of universal deceit, telling the truth is a revolutionary act."

There is another truth teller among us whose name we will soon speak in the same breath of other truth tellers like Viola Davis and Malcolm X. A sage, a 'round-the-way' brother in these streets who calls it like he sees it. This new truth teller is Theo E.J. Wilson. His new book, *The Law of Action*, is a virtual treatise to truth telling, as well as homage to the processing of living your truth; action. This is one of those books you'd like to force-feed to every activist, civic leader, working man or woman and do-gooder who has ever talked about doing something positive in the world, but somehow got stuck in the muck and mire of everyday living. Don't get me wrong. Life is beautiful, even in the weeds, but Theo's book takes the Crayola 64 pack of the day-to-day and turns it into an amazing Technicolor Dreamcoat of possibilities.

The Law of Action is an inspirational read designed to

provide you with samples, solutions and a plan to make your personal dreams come true, and leverage those dreams to create a better world. It is written with a wink to the activist, but with a nod to all of us who know there has to be a better way than 'this.' As Wilson points out in the theme of the book, there is a *law* of action that has to ride shotgun with our lofty dreams as they speed down the road.

Wilson uses the canvass of his own life to paint a vivid picture of trial, error, success, and repeat. The story of his relationship with his Sensei is the one that some of us make up in our own minds when we wish to romanticize our life stories. Wilson actually has those stories to tell because he's lived them.

We used to call people like him 'Renaissance Men.' Men who were unafraid to live several lives in one life, and had the receipts to show for those experiences. The amazing thing about Wilson is that he has lived so much in a short period of time. This is the beauty of his book, *The Law of Action.* It gives us an in-real-time experience of the Renaissance masters at a young age. This way, we don't get the dreamy eyed wistfulness of an older person reminiscing of younger days.

This is not to discount any wisdom of his tales and insight. On the contrary, his uncanny ability to deliver wisdom with in-your-face realism makes it a book that delivers the goods with a smile. It provides proper decorum, but will punch you in the neck for good measure so that you don't get intellectually lazy and sleep on his knowledge. This is rare territory that few can travel. Wilson does it with the skill of wily veteran whom the rookies turn to when the battle is on the line.

I have watched Wilson over the years as an activist and have seen his commitment to doing the right thing. He did so even when the opportunity came for an easy out; to grab the low hanging fruit and call it a day. Theo is from a new generation of thought leaders that are asking a far deeper, basic question: "It is good that we are saving the babies from the river, but let's ask who is throwing the babies in the river upstream, and how do we stop it?" His book, *The Law of Action*, is a reflection of Wilson asking that basic question of himself, and now you, the reader.

The benefits of *The Law of Action* are legion, but allow me to name the ones that landed in my lap.

- It provides a level of encouragement in the face of discouragement, so you could call it a motivational read.

- It provides a mystical look inside of Wilson's soul so that we can put ourselves in that place, and do our own spiritual discovery.

- It provides clarity of thought so that we're not caught up in trying to figure out what the writer is saying.

- It provides practical tools for us to create a real-world plan of action to move beyond our current plateaus.

- It provides an honest look at a person who walked through dark nights of the soul, and how to effectively utilize those experiences for our own good, as well as the greater good.

There's something here for everyone...if you're strong enough.

Truth and action are the Thelma and Louise of our day. But instead of a dénouement of a car driving over a cliff, Wilson shows us a new road forward – a bridge appears, using tools that make sense and actually change things. This is the first of Wilson's literary announcements to the world. Take the first step on this journey of a thousand, beginning with Chapter 1.

Chet W. Sisk
Social Futurist/Author of Above and Beyond All That We Know
Founder
LEAD Global.
www.leadtheshift.com

1: A QUESTION OF VIOLENCE

He stood on my goddamn stomach. My martial arts instructor made my abs his new floor boards as I held my feet six inches from the ground. I felt the roundness of his heels slip and settle into the crevices between my abdominal muscles. This 170-pound warrior tested my mental toughness. Dr. Abayomi Obadele Meeks looked like an older version of the rapper, Common, but with a full head of locs. He was an East Coast transplant with a speech pattern that incidentally mimicked Denzel Washington's, so when he spoke we listened. The man's chiseled frame and alarmingly fast reflexes were backed by an encyclopedia of martial wisdom. He held a Ph.D. in Chinese medicine, and was a practicing acupuncturist by day. This meant that his knowledge of the human nervous system was staggering, and he knew precisely how to either heal or destroy with it. He was absolutely devastating, and standing on my fucking stomach.

This Saturday was like so many others at the Moyo N'Guvu Cultural and Healing Arts Center; action-packed. It was hit-or-be hit. I used to think to myself during training, "Either you take action, or action takes you." We did combat drills, learned new moves, and sparred exhaustively under the tutelage of the fiercest man we knew. Dr. Meeks was a master-level instructor in the African martial art of Kupighana Ngumi, a Swahili word which means, "to use the body as a fist." It can best be described as Krav Maga meets Thai Boxing meets Capoeira. I remember the African drum being a constant teaching tool. Its rhythm provided the backdrop to us literally dancing the fight moves into our muscle memory. This was to ensure that when faced with real-world combat, we wouldn't have to think: our bodies would win the fight for us. I remember this being a painful process at times. Truthfully, Dr. Meeks didn't give a shit about discomfort in his students, short of what would lead to permanent injury. This meant temporary injury was on the table for instructive purposes. Something in me appreciated that. The man was rigorous and exhausting, like real fights often are. He began to literally instruct class from the pedestal of my solar plexus. My core began to vibrate as the first signs of fatigue set in, struggling to keep my feet elevated and legs extended. The unpadded carpet floor was no help in this process. He felt the trembling in my stomach, and began a new paragraph, laughing and seemingly oblivious to my pain. I slowly tuned him out, escaping within as his words faded away, meditating on images of iron. I envisioned my stomach to be a reinforced pillar of steel, undaunted by the weight of mere human body. I had gotten good at this. Violence was a reality that I embraced early in life, a trait Dr. Meeks and I had in common.

I retreated deep within myself. My mind, the only sanctuary from my compromised physical body. Suddenly, Dr. Meeks yelled "Sita," the Swahili command for "finished," and stepped off of my stomach. By this time, I was so deep into meditation, I almost missed the command. I slowly relented as he looked me in the eye with a glint of proud approval, and moved on with the rest of the class.

It was 2006, and I was deep into my spiritual journey. Along with martial arts practice consuming my free time, I studied the highest philosophies the corner bookstore could keep in stock. Shining Lotus was a metaphysical gift shop that looked like the Hogwarts library in real-life. Walking in there felt like stepping into an embassy from Heaven, a celestial outpost on a dirty urban intersection. Browsing the DVD section, I stumbled upon a movie called, *The Secret* and I inquired about the content. The shop owner spoke about it like a crack dealer with new product on the street, all quiet and excited about the results. I bought it and raced home. Sitting in front of my TV, I popped it into my PlayStation 2 with anticipation of my life being changed.

At first, I was enthralled. Had I really been making this journey too damn hard? Was positive thinking and emotional preparedness a muscle that I had undertrained? Was poverty simply a defect of the mind? I said out loud to the television, "So let me get this straight. All we have to do is willfully focus on the things we want and not the things we don't and eventually, we'll be living our dreams?" It felt good, and sounded even better. But, over the weeks, something would begin to nag me to no end.

America was in the midst of George W. Bush's war in Iraq. CNN and FOX News pumped news of American casualties and a rising civilian death toll on a seemingly endless loop. There were reports that American soldiers had been firing depleted uranium shells, causing untold health issues to unborn Iraqi children. This caused epic cognitive dissonance with what I was learning from this new "Law of Attraction" teaching. So, I had to ask, "What about all the bad shit in the world? What about Fallujah, Rwanda and Beirut?" America was wreaking havoc on innocent people all across the world, and the global protests didn't seem to matter. It dawned on me that America wouldn't even be here had it not been for the genocide of the Indigenous that cleared the land we built our highways, Wal-marts, and airports on. God dammit, what about the Indians?

I just couldn't make sense of it. The genocide of the Native Americans baffled me to sleeplessness, literally night after night. According to *The Secret* and other Law of Attraction teaching, they were doing everything right. In the movie, they mentioned that the first Indigenous Americans could not even see the ships of the Spanish because they had no frame of reference for their shapes. If this is so, then they also had no frame of reference for the brutality they would soon suffer. Darn it, why hadn't *The Secret's* producers also mentioned the violence the Indigenous Americans suffered? How could they just glance past that glaring reality for the sake of making this movie? What negative thinking must the Indians have been doing to attract their destruction? What an unfair assumption. It was as if the authors of *The Secret* movie and the book had no concept of people being the recipients of real-word violence. That certainly would benefit the people in Iraq whom we were launching missiles at. There had to be another level of spiritual reality to explain things like massacres, child molestation and carpet-bombings. Unsolicited violence is a real thing, and it was what I was training myself to defend against at Moyo Nguvu. Some people are itching to destroy other people, and nobody knew this like the America's First Peoples. How were they to comprehend the far-off inner workings of European civilization? The whole, "Either you take action or action takes you," ethic seemed to permeate the Zeitgeist of Europe's age of empire. The wars, the famines, the plagues that shaped Europe into the technological powerhouse it became were as far from their consciousness as the workings of some alien civilization is to ours.

This whole law of attraction thing began to seem fishy to me. According to the teachers of this "Secret" doctrine, you supposedly only attract what you focus on and give emotional energy to. Well, if this "law" were so universal, Indigenous genocide would have been impossible. An injustice of the scale should have been universally, 'illegal.' By and large, a harmonious civilization thrived here on the American landmass prior to Cristobol Colon's voyage across the waters in 1492. They had sustainability, matriarchal gender equality, open borders for immigrants, and a constitution in the Iroquois Federation of Nations. No words for "prison industrial complex", and "rape culture". No words for, "war on drugs", and "nuclear disarmament." Peaceful, in tune with nature, focused on the positive: that's the general consensus on the "Indians."

Many say that we romanticize the Indigenous of the Americas. If so, it was European authors who began that romance. Bartolome De Las Casas, who first voyaged to the new world in 1498, wrote of the Indigenous tribes of the Caribbean Islands with glowing astonishment. In his famous manuscript, *A Short Account of the Destruction of the Indies,* he said, "Of all the infinite universe of humanity, these people are the most guileless, the most devoid of wickedness and duplicity." In fact, his affection for the natives of the Americas was great enough for him to take action against Columbus, and become a whistle-blower for the atrocities committed on the expedition. There was only one problem; he suggested that Africans replace the Natives in the labor force of the New World. The Catholic Church agreed. Thus began the journey of my ancestors to the Americas.

The slavery experience was a terrifyingly awful, yet an effective display of action at work. Exercising the brutality necessary to capture and enslave other human beings is calorically expensive. The boats to ship them weren't going to build themselves. The iron for the shackles wasn't going to smelt itself. America grew strong on the rippling shoulders of Africans working themselves to death. Skeletons of slaves bear the tell-tale signs of ligaments torn from the bones because their body gave out beneath the crushing weight of the work. I see my ancestors lifting repeatedly, dragging and sweating, building the economic equivalent of the great pyramids. That is to say, the raw physical power necessary to construct the American economy from scratch is something the world is likely never to see again. In a gut-wrenching way, it is a marvel; a marvel that too many descendants of these slaves are still excluded from enjoying the full fruits of. Sadly, America has yet to live up to the promise of liberty and justice for more simply than a few.

So, what the heck? How could the universe allow this to happen to the Native Americans. Peaceful, loving, civilized...and still driven to the brink of extinction? Were the settlers being right about, "Manifest Destiny?" This narcissistic idea that Europeans were to take this new world and 'tame' it was responsible for the kidnaping of my forbearers from Africa and enslaving them here as well. If Manifest Destiny were valid, that would mean these atrocities were also justified, and all efforts to resist conquest and end slavery were thereby, immoral. Well, to me that thought was utterly absurd.

Fortunately, the Indigenous and Africans are resilient beyond measure. Perhaps this kind of intestinal fortitude is what Dr. Meeks was cultivating in me. We quickly learned the warfare tactics of our colonizers and won a great many battles, though many were erased from history. The Lakota victories in the Black Hills are slated as the first true military defeats suffered by the United States Army. From the Seminole wars in Florida, to Palmares in Brazil, the Native Americans and Africans resisted and fought for their lives. This warfare was largely erased from history, but the effects linger to this day. Because they adapted effectively, colonialization had to change its tactics. On one hand, the indigenous people of America have been nearly eradicated. Viewed from another angle, they are far from extinct. A recent genetic study of the mitochondrial DNA of Mexican women showed that 80% of them are actually of indigenous matriarchal lineage. This means that genetically speaking, Mexicans, the secondlargest ethnicity in America, are truly Native Americans. Their numbers are not dwindling, but growing, much to the chagrin of the far-right wing in this country. Add that to the countless millions of 'Mestizos' throughout Central and South American, and you've got a majority in the western hemisphere. The tide is turning, indeed.

But why did this have to happen in the first place? Why wasn't the balanced and harmonious nature of the Indigenous and African peoples enough to prevent all of this? A scary reality seems to underlie the universe we live in. Violence, destruction, and death are woven into the fabric of existence, our ethics be damned. Either through natural unfoldment or forceful destruction, all lifeforms are destroyed. Dr. Wayne Dyer once remarked that if the world was fair, the bird would never eat the worm, for the worm had not "deserved" to die. The human moral standard of "fair" seems to be a fabrication. There is a part of this universe that is wholly amoral and indifferent to our suffering. It just doesn't weigh death and its causes on the same moral scale that man does. Chaos, mayhem, and violence exists whether man does or does not, and are preeminent over our judgement of their blind, brutal force. Planets get hit with asteroids all over the universe. Baby animals are eaten within hours of their birth if their mother cannot protect them from the lions, the wolves, or the orcas. Volcanoes erupt and smother innocent civilizations; man, woman, and child be damned.

I believe this understanding is why Dr. Meeks was so hard on us. He who strikes first and hardest most often survives. Either you take action, or action takes you. African martial arts have a brutality proportioned to that which was shown unto our people. We did cartwheels through fields know to have thorns until the skin on our palms thickened. I punched boards, metal pillars and concrete until my knuckles grew beneath the skin. We trained hand-drills, sparring, and combat combos until we bled, all because he realized that nothing about existence is inherently fair. He was ruthless to within the confines of what the law would allow him to do in order to prep us for utter lawlessness. Perhaps a time would come where we would have to be a law unto ourselves. After all, it seems that we humans hold these same raw natural powers within us. Perhaps, man is endowed with the ability to accelerate natural forces, positive and negative. We humans harnesses the preexisting tendencies of the universe for creation, and yes, destruction. Since matter and energy can be neither created nor destroyed, does it really 'matter' to the universe if a life form is dead or alive? One could argue that does matter to the universe since life is even possible in the first place. However, it seems that nature delights in destruction as well.

The scientific community has taken note. Dr. Neil Degrasse Tyson said during a lecture in Walla Walla, Washington in 2012, "When I look at the universe and see asteroids coming down to strike and rendering species extinct, I see forces of nature that would just as soon have us dead or extinct, I don't see the goodness in the world that people speak of." This is an apt observation. Everything must die for something to keep living. Whether eating grass or one's own cubs, predation is built in the fabric of biology. It is a great motivator for movement. Why would the Zebra even run if not for the lion, and vice versa? Why wings instead of fins? Why evolution at all were the threat of death not ever present?

Action is a life or death affair. With no form being sacred in the eyes of existence, if any form cannot preserve its life...then it won't be a form for long. Why does the bird eat the worm? Because it can. Why did the Europeans attack the civilizations of Native America? Because they could. Why did they kidnap my ancestors from Africa into the belly of ships to be sold as property in the new world? Because it was a possibility in the universe, and action was taken to do so. Ouch.

Wouldn't it be nice if the way things are in this world just happened to fit neatly into our moral code? Certainly, it would. The fact that brutality can be committed doesn't mean it is right to do so. Just because a man can physically dominate a woman and violate her doesn't mean it's right to do so. Completely the opposite is true. He is not more valuable because he's physically stronger. The knowledge in her head and in her experience, could very well be the cure to what makes him feel compelled to attack. Similarly, just because Europe had the military might to conquer native America did not make it a better civilization. Quality of life, sustainability, longevity, and spiritual wellbeing are measures we could clearly say the indigenous people vastly outperformed Europe. We put moral codes in place to preserve this very possibility. We craft codes of conduct because the true value of human potential could possibly be lost if we allow raw, lawless violence to smother our inner gifts.

Yet, it is us humans alone who civilize the brute violence of the universe. We have the mental capacity to deny our base instincts for the preservation of human potential, and for good of all life. Perhaps 'evil' is the human predator instinct, misdirected. The fact that some people prey on other humans is unsettling. Upon observation, it seems that unevolved people hunt and trap things other than the flesh of our fellow humans. Sometimes, intangible things whet non-physical appetites. Some of us take pleasure from watching pain, so the suffering of others becomes the 'prey.' Predation seems to be the loophole in universal law of attraction. It is as unfair as a factory farm. Why do they exist? Because they can. They exist because they are possible, and the chickens, cows, and sheep and pigs lacked the actionable power to stop it. We do, and we must.

This was a chilling realization. Murder exists because it is a precondition for eating, which all organisms must do. Can nations be classified as macro-organisms? Can giant, hive-minded collections of humans become like ants and take resources from nations who lack the actionable force to deter them? The blunt answer is, yes. It's undeniably morally wrong, yet universally possible, and so the possible takes precedence over the proper. Ask any other creature in the food chain how unfair this world is. 'Action' takes them constantly if they get caught slipping. Any nature documentary will demonstrate this occurrence on land, sea, and in the air. What pretense does man entertain that he should somehow escape such a fate for all time?

To prevent this terrifying occurrence, men like Dr. Meeks raised armies. Warrior cultures have existed for thousands of years. Since the first bands of men accepted saber tooth tigers as an inevitable factor of life, armed groups of homo sapiens have conditioned themselves to draw blood, and to do so unflinchingly. In pockets of the planet where human-on-human predation seemed a given, the tools of violence advanced accordingly. They needed to fend off the most advanced predator of all time, and hopefully turn their predator into prey. The only moral was survival, and all other values were ordered beneath it. To survive, you needed to take action. Action fires the neurons that move the muscle into involuntary fight or flight. Therefore, action is hardwired into the central nervous system. Our cells anticipate the evasion or the committing of violence for survival, because violence is...action.

To me, it was becoming clearer. In a universe that allows possible predation upon all of its creatures, it is suicidal to leave out violence as a part of one's moral map. Maybe, it is there to inform us of the perishability of the fragile form we all inherit at birth. Survival drives us all into action. Whether it be running, fighting, eating, or mating, action is the result of inescapable and self-enforcing powers. Therefore, action is necessarily a law. The law of action is the law of survival in and of itself. It's not that violence is always necessary, but that violence is an action, and action is necessary for survival. It's so obvious, yet so overlooked that it is never properly examined.

However, the American empire built on the bones of the natives has come to an interesting crossroads. This culture now takes action to the point of imbalance. This busy-body ethos perfected by Europe is the foundation of the modern world. Working for a living, paying rent, industrial resource exploitation are all holdovers from feudalism. But where are we going with all of this? Everybody must have money to live. All of us must take action to get it. With the exception of the super wealthy, humans are still in do-or-die mode to make ends meet. All this action creates products, which produces waste, and the resources of the planet are consumed for the exchange of a manmade fiction called money. Have we lost the meaning behind the motion? Is survival a good enough motive, or was the universe teaching us something else all along? Is there a way to engage in action that is effective, and does not add further pollution to the ego-saturated planet we share? In a culture that was built on the destruction of the Native

Americans, we must learn to think like Indigenous people in order to survive. How Ironic.

Now is the time we figure this out. No time has there ever been more at stake for humans and for the other species on earth. It appears our action has taken the world to the brink of destruction, but our inaction will insure that it falls. This is not a problem we can pray our way out of. The people most effected must do something, and do it effectively. The good thing is that the universe is always in motion; action is never 'not' happening, proving that if you don't take action, it will certainly take you. Now, how do we act in accordance with the game? How do we accelerate the healing of this world? The game isn't over yet, even for the poorest among us. Let's take a look at the laws that set our being into motion, and examine how to master these forces.

2 KARMA: MASTERING THE ECHO

Newton's second law of motion states, "The acceleration of an object as produced by a net force is directly proportional to the magnitude of the net force, in the same direction as the net force, and inversely proportional to the mass of the object." In layman's terms, for every action, there is an equal and opposite reaction. This is clear when it comes to bouncing balls and inanimate objects, but what about the events of life? How do we apply these principles in a practical manner?

You've heard the term, "What goes around comes around." This describes what some would call karma. The term, karma, has taken on a mostly punitive connotation. We wish for evil-doers to get their "karma" and be punished for their crimes. We believe that good, helpful actions should somehow be returned to us in life. However, in its original language of Sanskrit, karma literally means "action." That's it. What we are wishing on evildoers is for the fruits of their actions to return to them like Newton's laws of motion say that they should.

In our real lives, it's a little more complex than that. The action that we take cannot go nowhere. Things we set forth come back to manifest in our lives, but there seems to be a delayed reaction. Similar to standing on the lip of a cliff and screaming into a canyon, it takes a while for what we set forth to come back. How fast it returns is based on the size and depth of the echoing medium. Perhaps life is the biggest echo chamber we know.

In my life as an activist, I got quite familiar with delayed reactions. In late 2004, a coalition of young

Black social justice advocates decided to form a coalition called "the C.O.R.E," the Colorado Organization for Racial Equality. Our first project was not slaying some external dragon threatening the Black community, but to address our problems within. An idea was born called "Barber Shop Talk." The idea was simple yet ingenious; We would use the barber shops in the neighborhoods to hold organized community forums, reaching the people exactly where they were. It took off, and our president at the time, Olajde Gamu, made the connections to start the forum. Olajide was the son of a black American mother and a Nigerian father. He was mercurial, clever and charismatic. We got along well, and because of my background in performance and public speaking, he chose me be the main facilitator.

We printed flyers, and just went. Our street team attended other community forums held by other organizations, and advertised after contributing. Hitting the ground running alleviated any jitters that we had because we simply didn't have time to entertain them. We picked every other Wednesday, because why the hell not? Montbello Barbers agreed to host us, and they turned their resources to making sure we were successful. The community responded well. We collected emails, shook hands, and engaged. We had separate men and women's forums. This was because both genders felt more comfortable expressing themselves absent the eyes and judgement of their counterparts. Just like that, we had a movement.

About a year in, we lost steam and momentum. Talking in barber shops was okay, but we did not yet know how to translate it into action. People needed to feel like they were improving something, not just chewing the fat. We didn't necessarily know what we were doing, and with only a few connections and no knowledge of the non-profit and activist landscape, the attendance dwindled. Olajide joined the air force and the group fell apart. To my knowledge, we were done.

Then, seven years later out of the blue, Olajide reached out to me. He had moved to Washington D.C. for the armed services, and there he had been rebuilding the organization, unbeknownst to me. He had a whole new crew of brothers and was preparing a conference call for them to meet me. He wanted me to be chief facilitator and mentor for a now national organization. My immediate task; rebuild Barber Shop Talk in Denver. The echo had returned.

One of the members of the C.O.R.E. organization, Shwanna House, had gotten married since then. She had been a quiet background force in the early days, making sure our "I's" were dotted and "T's" were crossed. Shwanna had been a singer in town with a band called "Sweh." I had gone to see her once or twice, but she slowly faded into memory. Well, now Shwanna House was Shwanna Hines. Her husband, Quincy Hines, had a passion for social justice. He had a great deal of raw energy and passion, and was simply looking for a target to aim it at. He would be my right-hand man, and I his, as the mission to awaken the people was once again at hand. Quincy and I started the process from ground up, going to forums and attending workshops in the community, putting our organization out there. Little did we know, it was exactly what the community desired; a place where they could just tell the truth in the open, a place like Barber Shop Talk. Seemingly out of nowhere, the attendees from the old forums appeared, telling us they had missed the organization, and they were ready to get involved. This time, there was grant money available. This time, we would build the bridges that would lead from talking to action in the community. The organization revived itself and in short order, we were back on track.

Manifestation is like growing a garden. Events don't just occur; they begin as seeds and flourish in the delay of time. It takes action to get action. What we've put out into the lives of others takes on a life of its own. In this way, people are each a unique echo chamber, a unique garden. How fast or slow we get back what we put out often depends on how fertile they are to the law of action. These actions can cascade over many people like the wave in a stadium, or come back automatically given the receiving persons tendency to reciprocate your energy. Either way, positive or negative, what we do always goes somewhere.

The most tedious part of life is the delay, the lag time, between the original action and the echo returning. This can be the most deceptive part of life for both the actor and the receiver. Some echoes only linger a second. Others linger for centuries. Some echoes cascade down through generations upon generations of people. In this way, everything we do absolutely matters. Due to the law of 'karma' or action, we all imprint on eternity forever. If our lives never make the news, whether we live as hermits or heroes, the fact that we took up space and used this planet's resources makes a mark. It cannot not be this way. Once we exist, once our mothers take up nine months of resources to nurture and birth us, we are an investment of the universe. Your life will leave a mark, large or small. The delay just makes this hard to see at times.

Changing the direction of one's life is simply a matter of sustaining the desired echoes for long enough to outlast the return of the undesired ones. Ignorance of this fact is why so many people, for example, struggle to escape street life, or addictions. The about-face of leaving the "thug life" is often made amidst times of great turmoil and trauma. Some people die before they can escape. Depending on how violent or active the participant in street life was, it could be a while before the echoes die down. It could be what you set forth in the lives of rivals, of old connections, of the opinions of an obsolete peer group that returns to cancel out the echo of your new direction. You must persist in new action, anyway. If safety is an issue, one may have to take the action of relocation to weather the storm of karma. This would be a new echo. Persistence in a new chain of events, in planting a new harvest, is essential to the mechanics of change.

The ancient Egyptians referred to the earth realm as "Geb." Geb was a word that sometimes doubled for "womb." The events of space-time gestate like a pregnancy. When they are fully formed, they manifest as an event. The realm of Geb is what many scientists call, the fourth dimension. What is waiting in the womb of space-time to be birthed into your life? What seeds have you planted there? These karmic echoes can shape the fate of future generations.

For example, my father's decision to move to Denver from New York directly impacted my destiny. He took action, and that action took my life in an alternate direction. His decision chose my mom, it chose the atmosphere and therefore my friends, the teachers I met, mountains I could visit readily and the ocean I could not. And my father is the echo of his predecessors moving from Jamaica to New York, and so forth. Though this is obvious to a certain level, one cannot overlook the significance of these acts. Wielding this intentionally can give one tremendous power. The hand of the past writes the present. Now, what will you write into the future?

Whose echoes are you holding? What chain of decisions are you keeping in motion? What effects are you continuing to cause? Are you even the source of your behavior, or did someone write the script for your actions? Questions like this lead to the necessary self-examination to be a cause in our world. This is where freedom lies. Nothing is like the feeling of setting forth the forces that liberate your karma, and therefore your destiny.

When viewed from the perspective of an echo chamber, karma loses its punitive sting. Often, we imagine that we live under this divine crime-and-punishment set up when it's actually a little less personal than that. The universe isn't out to get you, it's out to teach you. It's there as a process of unfoldment that is highly ordered, even when appearing chaotic. One never knows the milieu of circumstances, personal issues, missed opportunities, and greater good outcomes attached to seemingly random tragedies. Nor do we know the investment, sacrifice, and hidden causes behind seemingly lucky breaks we see other people getting. What is for certain is that all events, whether positive or negative, have been gestating in the womb of space-time often far longer than it took them to occur in real time.

It's the imagination that imposes the judgement of 'blessing' or 'curse' onto the events of our lives. Sometimes, the imagination has been fueled by years of religious belief that reinterpret occurrences into stories that fit a person's paradigm. This, more often than not, leads to problems in effectively rooting out the true causes of many religious people's problems. In my life, for example, I found the belief that someone else could pay the price for my personal sins extremely harmful. If I could not be saved from physics itself, who would save me from cause and effect? Perhaps it appeared I got spared from some greater harm because I was *told* that whatever penalty for my misdeeds should've been harsher. This did not change the fact I was sole author of the events in question. Once I got out of religion, I saw a how much mental chatter the institution cloaked over raw physical facts of believers' lives. This cloak of mental chatter imposed seemingly imaginary dictates, reinforced by group-thinking, over very simple and obvious issues that could be overcome with critical thinking and common sense action.

The facts are the facts. We have a shared, objective reality so that we can have something to check the errors of our mind against. Thank goodness. Our lives are on a one-way track. We cannot go backwards and undo our past. Some of us would like to for the sake of correcting mistakes. The issue with that is that if we could go backwards, we may well also undo our good deeds. They too are registered into the halls of eternity, never to be changed or erased. The only tools we have are the present moment, and a mind that can study the past, the present, and plan for the future. The future is just the 'now' that hasn't happened yet. I find it profoundly simple that one can actually set up and predict the future like dominoes to some extent. For example, I predict an on-time departure to work, so I'll set up the future by putting my keys in a place I can find them. I'll set up the morning by having my clothes ironed tonight, my car full of gas and breakfast premade. Simple. However, simple actions like this move other events in motion like you looking sharp in the eyes of your peers at work and then getting a promotion which gets more money which changes your destiny, etc. What a profound echo from something so painfully simple. Consciously set up the dominoes in your life. Understand the impersonal nature of the echo chamber. Many things are not in your control, but the things that are will have reverberations that begin to shape the larger flow of events in your favor. When we get conscious about this principle, patient about the turnaround time, we microscopically start to master our universe.

It must be said and acknowledged that we swim in a sea of other people's echoes. You could be impeccable with planning to get to work on time, and an accident up the road will stop traffic. You could plant the perfect vegetable garden for the fall harvest, and the neighbors' dog gets loose and tears up your crop. These events can suck, but they do keep life interesting. They also are great at teaching you about other people, your environment, what you should, and should not do. Just know that there won't be an accident every day going to work. The dog may or may not tear up the garden. What's more important is that this principle makes you a master of your internal space rather than a micromanager of your external world. That only leads to compulsion and insecurity which is counterproductive. The goal is to put you in the driver's seat when it comes to the unfoldment of the events in your life. Understand the time delay of the echo. Develop the patience to sustain new action through the reverberations of your old ones, and watch your situation transform.

3 HABIT AND THE BODY COMPUTER

Human beings are wonderfully complex. However, these big brains and wild hearts of ours can possibly be a combustible recipe. How do we balance so many intricate functions without driving our lives off the proverbial cliff? Fortunately, we have a system of automation built into us. There is a fantastic symphony of nano-machinery wiser than we can comprehend, and it is running our bodies non-stop. It is an astounding teacher, and an even better learner. We can tap into this intelligence and program some of the body's functions for our favor. We call this programming, *habit*. Habit evolved to free up brain matter to learn new things, and made mastery possible in multiple areas at a time. In this way, when we take action, the body can take it over and over again without thinking. Sadly, when programmed incorrectly, habit is the bane of our existence. It becomes the single greatest obstacle to obtaining all that we desire and combined with the echo principle, can send out lives into a tailspin without us knowing how to stop it.

We have seen this so many times in the realm of celebrity gossip. Some megastar can't quite get their behavior under control and loses their fans, opportunity, and sometimes their very lives. We sit back in awe at how their sheer humanity erases the glamour of their celebrity. How come they just can't get it right? After all, look at the incentives. For a paycheck that size, it seems as if you'd have all the motivation in the world to change. Add in the fact that there are millions, often billions of people watching, and the situation becomes downright baffling. We grab our popcorn and watch it all go down in flames.

The truth is that no matter what scale we play the game of life on, the fundamental rules stay the same. Action repeated over time tends to stick. Neuroscience tells us that every behavior we take part in forms a groove in the brain's pathways. The more we repeat an action, the deeper the groove becomes. If a habit becomes too deeply ingrained, willpower alone is rendered insufficient to reverse the pattern. This ability to change the brain is referred to as "neuroplasticity." Once it is set in motion, it can be a herculean task trying re-write the coding typed into our cells.

I struggled with this fact in my own life. Losing weight and getting lean was an uphill battle that literally consumed me. Hour upon hour, I obsessed over why my workouts weren't working. As it turns out, you can't outwork a bad diet. The issue was, I had no idea how bad my diet actually was. During my younger years, my metabolism was so fast and efficient, I didn't worry about my diet because if I wanted to change anything, exercise was enough. After hitting the age of 28, I witnessed a severe metabolic slowdown. My genetics had taken over my ambition. The men in my family are all strong and long-lived, but have a tendency to put on bellies with time. As an actor and performer, this was not the look casting directors were looking for.

Over time, I found intermittent fasting. This is when you only eat within a small window of time in the day, and the rest of the time, your metabolism burns fat for you. It literally took me years to master because I would interrupt my fasting cycle. Then, after moderate progress, I got serious. Learning to discipline my appetite consistently for four weeks straight gave me more progress with my body than those previous years for one simple reason. I firmly set the habit in place and my body remembered it. It was as if my entire body was a computer that needed a reset.

Willpower is not the be-all to end-all, but it is the beginning. A lot of self-help gurus have downplayed the significance of will in the ability to change one's life. People want some trap door or some hack to willpower because it's something that we all have struggled with. These new-aged gurus focus more on imagination and visualization instead. This is sexy and appealing to the average reader, but it does not tell the whole truth. Sadly, I am here to burst your bubble. Sorry kiddos, but there's no way around it. If you want real results, real change, you're gonna have to go get focused and get disciplined...but luckily, not forever.

The real secret is that you only need strong willpower in the beginning. People get frightened of change because they think they'll have to be arduous and restrictive their whole entire lives. Not true. You only need enough willpower to set the new behavior in motion, and then habit takes over from there. Ask any vegan, and they'll tell you that hamburgers were hard to live without, but only at first. When their bodies got used to the new food, they seldom miss the meat. When cravings do come up again, they know that they've already exerted enough will to turn away. But here's what many non-vegans do not realize; If they do end up relapsing into red meat, they get sick. Their stomach gets queasy and it starts to reject the meat. This is because over time, they have under-produced the enzymes necessary to break the meat down since they quit. Their bodies no longer remember meat as a friend, and rejects it.

Interesting how the body's chemistry has a programming to it as well. Most of the time, we think of the brain as the computer. The truth is that our entire bodies can be programmed by whatever we do on a consistent basis. Dieters know that the actual stomach as an organ can shrink over time. Smells and secretions can become more pleasant or unpleasant based on diet, drugs and emotions. These things leave a mark on the experience of the owner of the body. In my case, I liked the feeling of lightness and buoyancy that intermittent fasting gave me. Intermittent fasting is a dieting technique that has you eating all your calories for the day in a small window of a few hours per day. The rest of the day is spent on an empty stomach, letting your metabolism eat your fat. I remember getting a food craving outside of my window, and just not wanting to experience the heaviness in my gut that would have come along with it.

Of course, nothing succeeds like success. Not only does the mind enjoy the visible effects of improving the body, but so does the body itself. Fitness gurus have described what's called a "set-point." This when the body 'remembers' a new normal. The secret behind the set-point lies in cellular death and rebirth. When you keep your body the same size for a long enough time, the cells reproduce in that exact position, cementing that shape into place. We see this in people who lose weight after being vastly overweight for some time. The skin doesn't shrink because it has a memory. The cells reproduced to hold the larger shape in place. You can use this for your advantage. In order to do this, one must change the expectations of their fitness goals and the time it will take to truly achieve them. If you're looking to diet and workout to go back to your old habits, you can kiss the reset goodbye. The reprogramming of the mind-body will be horribly unsuccessful if you can't wait to get back to what you used to do and eat. Rather, it is best to eat and exercise like the person you will become, not who you already are. With that approach, the body you want will simply emerge due to new habits. Over time, the new ideal you will emerge because you inwardly behaved as that person until they showed up visually.

This is the positive power of habit. It is rarely talked about, but needs to be discussed. We have the opportunity to automate the most difficult things in our lives, and make them second nature. No other creature exhibits this ability to the level of the human being. Through the power of habit, we can command our own evolution, inwardly and outwardly. I want you to take a second and imagine the most difficult thing in your daily routine. Whether it be getting up early for work, controlling your temper or sex drive, any addiction you cannot get a handle on, whatever. It's important to throw away any notion that you are cursed with this affliction. It's time to see it as an opportunity. The psycho-somatic computing mechanism that challenges you so much was actually meant for your good, and you can turn it around. But either you take action, or action takes you.

What about repeated failure, you say? Many of us, myself included, have been wracked by numerous attempts to achieve the ideal body-mind only to be thwarted by no one but ourselves. Talk about pigging out on vacation.   One week visiting my friends in Tallahassee put me back a month in training.   I have known frustration to the point of tears over a physique that seemed like it would forever escape me.   Those failures left a mark.   Little did I know, so did the successes.   Over time, incremental improvements impacted my journey, and were able to lead me back to where I had fallen from.   It turns out that successes created a memory, too.   In those moments of despair, and there were many, I began to count up all the times I had executed on my vision of a better body.   The thought dawned on me that every pushup, every mile I ran, every squat or deadlift was still with me.   What would my body be had I *not* burned those calories?   The answer; a heck of a lot further from my goal than I am right now.   On that simple basis, I had to keep going.

My subconscious and cells knew exactly what was trying to be accomplished.   It was simply about giving them better tools to do their job.   I began to look up who had the same basic body as me, and how did they make progress.   What new eating habits would need to be formed to get myself out of this rut?   What discipline?   What resilience.   The most dangerous things in goal setting are those little thoughts that pop up and tell you, "Nice try.   You suck.   Epic failure is your middle name!"   Even that has a chemical signature.   Even my thought life was effecting my body.   The negative self-talk in my brain would run rampant.   Our brains consume 20% of our body's energy, and that is a lot of wattage to power the "I suck" radio station.   It broadcasts stress hormones all throughout my body, which hold onto fat, the very thing I am trying to rid myself of.   The neuro-chemical soup we swim in programs the receptor cites on our very cells. What they do and don't take in has a lot to do with what they are used to, and that means the environment your emotions create.

When I realized that my longevity was being effected by my thoughts, I began to watch them like a hawk. Nothing became more important to me than *not* ingesting any more stressful thoughts than a situation called for. That included being mindful of how deep I let a situation affect me in relationships, and being mindful of the news I entertained. Social media pages had to be selectively viewed based on my emotional triggers. When I became aware of the link between my fitness and my thought life, I got extremely conscious about what I mentally consumed. Positive and affirming videos and podcasts, motivational speeches from various gurus became some very sought after content. The week I put this together in my head, I tried to literally overdose on positivity. My Youtube feed was all Les Brown, Tony Robbins, Brian Tracy and Andy Andrews. Fitness advice from Brandon Carter to the Hodge Twins, Cali Muscle to Kinobody. It seemed necessary to pump my brain full of a bunch of "You can do it!"

Something had to counteract the voices telling me I'd live in a wack body for my whole life. No one was going to do this but me. Nobody cared like I cared. And, it was all so simple in the end. If I am what I eat, it must also apply to my mind. I could literally crash-diet my thought patterns into a new and better formation.

The mind and body both have patterns. Like a fountain, the body is always replacing itself while maintaining the same shape. Instead of flowing water, we are made of flowing cells, constantly cycling through birth and death over a seemingly invisible template.

Since our bodies are so dense, it takes a lot longer than a fountain to cycle. The average body replaces all of its cells, from atoms in your brain to your bone matter, in about seven to eight years' time. This means that if you died eight years ago, not an atom of what they put in the ground is what you're walking around with, today. The mind has this same quality, but our stream of thoughts can move faster than a fountain's stream of water. Therefore, we have to constantly insert new and positive things in the flow or else life, the media, and the environment will cycle negativity through, and this will eventually comprise its permanent shape.

The conscious mental diet effects the diet of the body, and therefore, its health outcomes. Ask a fitness competitor, athlete, or model and they will tell you of the mental toughness necessary for a powerful, beautiful body. What makes the results easier to achieve is when one accepts the rigors of these vocations as a part of life. For me, the fact that I was always building a new body was somewhat exciting. I saw it as a way to improve on an old model, to always be getting better and more proficient with time. Hell, I could reverse the hands of time if I was willing to sacrifice, so I did. Little by little, the 'me' I wanted began to emerge. At that point, what used to be rigorous was now attractive, magnetic, and dare I say addictive. It felt good knowing that I was improving with every meal, especially if my workout made me feel like I earned it.

I have heard it said that destinies are made not by one big decision, but by many small choices on a daily basis. With the habits that I acquired, those choices became effortless. Slowly, I began to see how my body and youth were being preserved in contrast to some of my peers. Working with youth, I must admit to feeling flattered when the kids underestimated my age. This trend extended to casting directors in local productions legitimately thinking they were casting a man in his late 20's, and never asking if I was older than 30 because the thought never occurred to them. To me, healthy exercise habits and eating were a small price to pay to sip from the fountain of youth.

Habits can do more than just reshape the body the body aesthetically, but also genetically. The field of Epigenetics studies the effects of consciousness on DNA. Dr. Bruce Lipton wrote about this extensively in his book, "The Biology of Belief." According to Lipton, experiences can activate or shut down certain genetic markers, and these genetic markers can be inherited by future generations. In chapter 7 of the book, Lipton talks about the role of parents as genetic engineers. Per his research, studies done on infants suggested that the prenatal environment effects their behavior greatly. Babies have an entire life in their pre-birth phase that they can carry with them after they take their first breaths. It appears that a child is born far more complex than a 'blank slate.' Lipton's research revealed that a mother's chemical environment due to her emotions bathed the fetus in certain hormones, making the baby more susceptible to the corresponding emotions throughout their lives.

Lipton's research was backed up by a 2013 study at Emory University that concluded that a father's experiences played a role in shaping the child's genetics, as well. The research duo of Kerry Wessler and Brian Dias published a peer reviewed article in *Nature Neuroscience* with their findings. The implications of this were profound for me. Per this research, the experience of slavery could be swimming around in my genetics somewhere because my ancestors went through it. Whatever habits and psychological limitations they had could be passed down to me. I wondered if I had activated that these memories unwittingly in some way. Does the sight of shackles and chains in a museum affect me differently than a White person, or even an African person born on the continent? I could only imagine, but never know for sure.

What became clear to me is that if experience programs genetics, I had better get to programming victory into my genes. The greatest gift the son of a slave could give to himself is the experience of being a king. Whatever the realm, whatever the field, I knew that I had to experience boundless freedom in some way, and preferably before I reproduced. Suddenly, the actions that I take and the thoughts I entertained became even that much more precious. "I'm not just doing this for me, but all those who will come from me," I thought. What a precious gift. What an exciting opportunity. Each moment became alive with opportunity to act in ways that would program me into limitlessness. Applying the law of action now became a gateway to the changing the fate of my descendants. I loved my arms, legs, face back, and all the parts of me that I took for granted in a whole new way. They were indeed gifts that were passed down to me on a cellular level from generations long gone. My task was to take this slave flesh and re-program kingliness back into its blueprint. How marvelous a lot in life? What an amazing time to be alive, with this new knowledge at my fingertips. I began the alchemy of achievement. Like

Paracelsus, my goal was to take these base elements and transform them into something higher. I was a caterpillar in charge of my own metamorphosis. Not just transformation, but transmutation was my new obsession. Experience was the secret code to the body computer, and action was the programming language.

4 THE PASSIVE SIDE OF THE WILL

"Just take the damn note, Theo! It doesn't matter what you intended to do. It's what we saw that counts, not what wanted to portray." Luther Wells was always pointed in his director's notes. I didn't know how to not take them personally, and defending myself constantly, denying his critiques. Acting classes at the Essential Theatre under his tutelage was the last place you wanted to 'play dumb.' His temper was as legendary as his skill. Looking back on Mr. Wells, being openly gay and Black in the hyper-macho times he was raised in would have given anybody an edge. I didn't appreciate this at the time. To me, he was bullying from his position of authority, the entire acting class putting my monologue under the spotlight because of his little "issues."

Underneath it all, I had only taken criticism from men who were "more manly" than me. Getting accurately analyzed by a gay dude twisted my 19-year-old male ego into a pretzel, and I think he knew it. Luther had a sixth sense for when he wasn't being respected. I grossly underestimated his will, and what life was teaching me through him. My only way out of this unnecessary embarrassment was total humility. I had to take the damn note. What my intentions were did not matter nearly as much as what the consequences were to my recipients. My read of the classic Hamlet monologue, 'To be, or not to be' was underwhelming and inauthentic. Yes, subjective perceptions of the audience could play a factor, but the consensus was accurate. The director was right. This would be the first of many contests of wills that Luther Wells would win against my ego.

I had no idea how invaluable "taking the damn note" would become in my evolution. Being self-aware enough to accept my effect on my environment, and even be held responsible to some degree, had me really examine my unconscious agreements. The passive side of my will was always in the forefront of my mind. These acting classes were not the first time I had been made aware that I could be held accountable for my unintended effects. It reminded me of what my father told me about being an innocent bystander; they didn't exist. This was a matter of survival in the streets, and you had to be aware of your surroundings at all times. If a stray bullet hit you, it means you stayed too damn long, in dad's world view. In both cases, unintended consequences counted more than your intentions, and this principle could be a life or death thing, not simply an acting note.

In leadership, the passive side of the will's consequences grow exponentially. The axiom, 'either you take action, or action takes you,' becomes far truer when people follow you, and you're in the driver's seat. If you're not careful then action, or lack thereof, can take you and your following where they don't wanna go. This reminds me of a little-known quote from a well-known man. "I cannot shake the feeling that I am integrating my people into a burning house." These were the words of Dr. Martin Luther King Jr. about one week before his death. They were uttered to the legendary crooner, Harry Belafonte, when he discovered King looking troubled, gazing out of a window in his home. The Vietnam War was in full swing, and King was questioning the moral compass of America; he wondered if it even had one at all. After images from the front lines were published in the press, the suffering of the Vietcong struck King as unnecessary, and an act of brutal cowardice. What did America truly have to gain from beating up on such a small country? Moreover, was integrating the Black community into such a morally bankrupt country a mark of being complicit with the corruption? Was the act of blending with America the act of agreeing with her, as well? I imagine all the marching, the water hoses, the arrests, and letter from a Birmingham jail, the death threats and the victories swirling around in Dr. King's head. Here was the de facto leader of black America wondering if he had just lead 22 million black Americans into alignment with the most destructive government on Earth at the time. Dr. Martin Luther King Jr, winner of the Nobel Peace Prize, questioned whether he'd led all these souls to be accomplices to war. Integrating black Americans into this society was ever more clearly a gamble, one that King would not live to see play out.

A person of King's conscience asks the hard questions of their actions. People like this, great people, wonder about not only what they are doing, but what are they allowing. They question the passive side of the will. So much of our examination of action delves into what we intend to make happen. A more thorough examination deals with what we allow to happen. My father used to tell my sister and I the old saying, "The road to hell is paved with good intentions." This was his way of saying that outcomes are the best way to measure your success, not what you meant to do. A great deal of that measurement comes from what we allow to happen. What was the final result? That calculation takes into account the environment and context for your behavior. Moreover, this question leads to the examination of what inaction does to us and those around us.

The people that surround us can draw us into their agreements, and the energy echoes that they create. I learned this lesson the hard way in the latter part of my teenage years. There was a time when my associates consisted of young men of the "thuggish" variety. I never considered myself a thug, but what they did, I did by proxy. This meant that whatever karmic echoes they had out there, I would passively be involved in whether I actively wanted to be or not. This manifested on a night when a friend of mines' enemies came to call. For the sake of anonymity, I'll leave names out of this recounting. The identities of the parties involved are still a volatile matter. However, I will say that I was an avid weed smoker at this time. I had just finished a joint and was a little higher than average. I rarely completed a joint by myself, but these brothas pushed me to my limits.

That night, I was smoking with a longtime friend of mine. A little after midnight, we got a call that our boy was in danger. A conflict stemming from a night club confrontation had escalated, and now there was about to be a fight. We went to his apartment only to find his enemies already there, banging on his door. There were five of them, and two of us. Somehow, the weed convinced us we could take them. Plus the friend who called us to let us know was supposed to be on his way. After an exchange of words, I remember throwing a punch. Sadly, the marijuana ruined my timing and I remember getting pummeled. The bottoms of shoes descending upon me, punches raining down, all in high definition, slow-motion, marijuana induced splendor. Any fighting skill I had was gone by the wayside when I was high, and I had to take the beat-down. I remember grabbing the leg of one of the guys beating me, hoping to at least give one guy something to regret. It happened to be the leg of the biggest guy in the crew. No luck. He stomped out of my grip and preceded with the jumping. I turtled up, hoping that nothing I received that night would be too permanent.

Luckily, it wasn't. The police showed up and they scattered like roaches. I didn't cooperate with their questions, and played dumb to the situation like any good 'hood boy would do. I blatantly denied knowing what happened with a trickle of blood visibly running out of my nose. The cops smirked, gave up, and exited the scene. I was left with a reality-check my ass almost couldn't cash. Not wanting to get into drama was not enough to prevent it. The people I was hanging around attracted it, and I had to take ownership of that. Though I could not change them, I had the choice to change my habits and environment. That was the beginning of the end of my relationship with them, and marijuana in general. I couldn't smoke without being paranoid, afraid that I would be ill-equipped to handle life if it all went south, again. It was a hard lesson, but slowly, it was clear that I had to actively do something else, or get sucked into more bullshit.

What I needed was a different set of friends who were engaged in other activities. This is because at the moment you're doing something, this conversely means you are not doing something else. Simple, right? Now that the obvious has been stated, truly investigate what this means. As I type this, I'm also not cruising the web, sleeping, wishing idly for my book to come out, or daydreaming. As I get this done, those things are not getting done. This in a productive example of the principle at work. Let's look at something a little closer to home.

Before writing this book, I would spend night after night going out and drinking. Then, night after night I'd come home no closer to my dreams than I was before I left the house. Though I did not *mean* to postpone, and possibly forever cancel the manifestation of this ideal, that's exactly what I was doing. Had I been a parent at that time, the hours I spent away from the house were hours I was spending not raising my child. Then the question becomes, "Who or what was I allowing to raise my child when I was not there?" Perhaps I'd hope they were sleep, but not be sure of it. At that point, my choice to have a little fun then becomes the choice not look after my kid. A night or two of this, and likely there'd be no harm, no fowl in the long term. Let this pattern become a habit, and a Pandora's box of unhappy incidents are likely to develop in my child's life due to my own negligence.

The fact is that the vast majority of the suffering we will incur in life happens on the passive side of the will. It's not that we wanted these bad things to happen, it's just that we didn't *not* want them to happen bad enough to prevent them. How many children got to this world on the passive side of their parent's will? There are so many accidental deaths every single year due to simple lapses in judgement. These lapses can either end lives, or turn them upside down. Humans are risk takers, and we take our chances with the strangest of things. It seems that we will be held as accountable for the actions on the passive side of the will more than the active side.

Here's a larger, more pressing example. Look at the environmental disasters we are facing because of our burning fossil fuels. Tons upon tons of carbon emissions burden the biosphere, and rain down onto us as catastrophes. Animals are being plunged into extinction, numerous ecosystems are in permanent decline. Yes, none of us drive cars specifically because we hate polar bears, and want to see them emaciated and starving. None of us board a jet because of our personal vendetta against the icecaps, and can't wait until they melt away, laughing devilishly at takeoff. And yet, this is the agreement we are also making when we are transported on machinery that burns fossil fuels. If this weren't the case, then it wouldn't be happening. Yet, the activity of billions of humans is making sure that the planet's carbon-carrying capacity dives past the tipping point, threatening our very survival. This is because convenience has captured our passive will. The unspoken agreement we make is that we are fine with destroying the planet at the sake of our expediency.

Our participation in the modern accoutrements of western society is by and large governed by corporations. We are in world that our ancestors would envy and be awe struck by, until they realized how little control we have. Most of us do not grow our own food. Why would we when the produce section can carry anything we desire. Pushing a grocery cart is a lot less strenuous than pushing a plow. We don't even really know how most of this wonderful technology works. The mechanics of a cell phone or a kindle reader are a mystery to most. Even our cars have centralized computers that would baffle the auto mechanics of the 70's. In the old days, when the most complicated thing in your house was a wood burning stove, learning repairs was a task that you could do almost intuitively. Ask me to fix a touchscreen or a gaming console, and you're out of luck...and I'm kinda smart.

We are indeed hostages to the will of the producers of technology. The time it would take to learn how this stuff works would take away from the 40-hour work week we participate in to make sure we stay out of the elements. We pay specific people to do all the hard work of supporting our 21st century lifestyle so we can go back to enjoying our gadgets. Simultaneously, we lose our autonomy when doing so. Since these technically sound people who keep our gadgets going seem to be benevolent, we allow them to proceed unchecked. Then, Edward Snowden leaks to the world that these devices are spying on us, and we say little to nothing. Part of it is the technophobia we have about the things we depend on. If we could just go into the device and disable the spying, we would. Since we can't, our outrage is marginal. We realized that convenience has cost us our privacy, and it's so scary, we don't know what to do about it, so we instead do nothing.

This examination of the passive side of the will comes at the height of the Black Lives Matter movement in America. There have been so many extra-judiciary executions at the hands of police by these same technological gadgets, people are finally asking some hard questions. These questions span from, "Is it getting more frequent, or are there just more cameras?" to "Is the very idea of police an idea that needs to be done away with?" These events have thrown me into an even deeper line of questioning. Being a black male, I fit the demographic of those targeted most by the "criminal justice system" if it can be called such a thing. I am a survivor of police brutality, my survivorship being a seemingly rare thing. This being so, I am not afforded the luxury of plausibly denying the racial undercurrent of these events. I take my ability to examine these occurrences as a life-or-death vocation.

Therefore, as history seemingly repeats itself I have to ask, "How did we allow this to happen?" The "we" I refer to is not just Americans, but more specifically the descendants of American slaves. African-Americans were the ones set to lose the most if Dr. King's aforementioned experiment in integration did not work. I wonder how he would view the events of today. What would King say about Philando Castille and Sandra Bland? What would he say to the mother of Tamir Rice and Mike Brown? How would King comfort the son of Alton Sterling and the sister of Terence Crutcher? Would he have been brought in to lead the marches in Ferguson, or quell the violence in Charlotte and Baltimore? How would King feel about the murder rates in Chicago, or Compton in the 90's? How would he view crack cocaine and the rise of gangsta rap? Moreover, would Dr. King lament the conditions that made the art form's creation necessary? I'm sure he didn't mean for any of this to happen.

For many of us, the house is indeed burning. From this vantage point, it seems as if those who integrated in the 60's set their children up to pay a cruel price for their gambit. The number of youth killed in gang violence in the 80's, 90's and 00's far exceeds the number killed by the Ku Klux Klan in the hottest days of Jim Crow.

Still, even that number is dwarfed exponentially by the number of blacks killed by chattel slavery itself. Professor Henry Louis Gates' most recent estimate is that approximately ten million Africans were imported into the new world to live and die as slaves. This does not count the millions who died in the disgusting conditions of the middle passage, and well as those whose bodies could not withstand the march from the interior to the coastline of Africa. This number does not include the countless millions who were born, lived and died as slaves over centuries in North, South and Central America, as well as the Caribbean. None of these plantations could have existed had the enslavers not cleared the land of its original inhabitants, the Native Americans, whom Bartolome De Las Casas so passionately defended. If we count the Africans killed by colonialism on the continent itself, including the ten million Congolese killed by King Leopold of Belgium alone, the picture for successful integration looks bleak.

What steps should Dr. King have taken to secure the lives of future generations of black people, then? What would sewing up the holes on the passive side of the will have looked like? At the time of the Civil Rights Movement, integration seemed the only viable option for success. Prior to that time, the doctrine of "separate, but equal" had proved a dismal failure for black people. Not due to any fault of their own, but due to the climate of racial terrorism under segregation. Many Americans, and people the world over, are ignorant of the prosperous black communities African-Americans had been forced to build under American Apartheid. After emancipation, black people held the vast majority of the skill-wealth of the country. Slaves not only picked cotton, but were carpenters, blacksmiths, farmers, and inventors. Booker T. Washington harnessed this skill-wealth, and fostered an "up-from-your-bootstraps" ethos in black America, accelerated by Marcus Garvey. By the late 1910's, prosperous black communities had popped up all over the country. Most notably was Greenwood, Oklahoma, otherwise known as "Black Wallstreet." The 1920's would see these communities burned to the ground and ghettoized by the Ku Klux Klan, accompanied by their angry white neighbors. These massacres were branded as "race riots," implying that the violence was a two-way-street. It was not, and history would proceed to wipe these incidents out of its pages.

Therefore, the only safe space for black people seemed to be among white people. This was only logical, since going back to Africa would have put them under another form of colonialism at that time, anyway. Because of this reality, I do not blame my ancestors for pushing to integrate the institutions of this society. When a "whites only" sign came down, and blacks were finally served, it was a clear marker of progress. When African-Americans began to make their mark in popular culture such as commercials TV shows, and musical success on MTV, the world appeared to have indeed changed for the better. This is the world I was born into in the 80's. The terror of the 1960's seemed a relic of the past, and I was allowed to believe in an America where all opportunities were possible for children of any race. This was an illusion I didn't want to let go of. Examination of evidence, as well as my own experiences of blatant racism exposed the notions of a post-racial America being nothing more than a marketing ploy.

Now that I have the inclinations of fatherhood and becoming a family man, I examine the passive agreements in my life like never before. Knowing what I know about this country, history, and our place in it is at times an unbearable burden. There are days when I realize why people do not seek knowledge, because once acquired, action is required. This can lead to an excruciating inquisition of the very limits of your capabilities as a person. Changing the human condition can appear to be a task so much larger than the span of our arms, yet it looms anyway, daring us to reach for a greatness we scarcely seem worthy of, never mind capable of attaining.

If you observe closely, life never stops giving feedback about your potential. Are you taking the damn note? Are you willing to account for the effect you are having on the world, whether you mean to or not? What is being left in your wake as you pass through the lives of others. Surely those around us bear the fallout of our actions but so will our descendants. They will inherit the fruits of not only what we did, but what we failed to do. So, I ask you, the reader, what will you do given your place in history? Using the events of the past as a contextual backdrop to the momentum of this moment, what are you willing to set in motion to improve our trajectory? It may not seem like it, but you can do something. Right here, in this present moment, you are alive and can do a myriad of things. Starting from right there in your body, the ability to sit or stand, to move forward or backwards, the capacity to read at all. Right now, cars are driving, planes are flying, signals are broadcasting and there you are. This moment that you are reading this is the furthest point in history. We are always poised on the cutting edge of world events with every moment. Each second is the crest of the wave that embodies the sum momentum of the universe from the big bang until now. You can lasso it like a bull and direct the flow. Do not allow yourself to sit passively, especially if negative events are in motion in your immediate sphere. To do so would be to agree with an outcome you could may not find pleasant, so get in gear and seize this opportunity.

5 THE MACHANICS OF MOTIVE AND MINDFULNESS

I used to love the Austin Powers movies. Mike Meyer's lovable spoof of the James Bond movies provided hours of entertainment. One thing that Austin said always stuck with me, however. "Wherever you go, there you are." To me, this means that there is ultimately no running from yourself, as there is no escape. Nothing reveals the truth about you like the results of the actions you take. Some outcomes are more unpredictable than others, but there are some ways to forecast results. It's about inner honesty. Being truthful about what's driving you can weed out certain undesirable results. Our state of being colors our actions whether we want it to or not. The inner quality of our mind while doing a task absolutely dictates the outcome. Mindful action is essential to success. It would be wise to check your heart before engaging a task, and study deeply your truest motivations. This reflection could save more time and energy than you can imagine.

During my time in undergrad, I saw this play out beautifully. I got my degree in Theatre Performance from Florida A&M University. At the time, it was the largest historically Black university in America, with over thirteen thousand students on a largely commuter campus. It was always magical watching the new students come in, especially being among them as a freshman. Soon, I got to know that there were two kinds of actors: the ones who loved the craft, and the ones who loved the spotlight. We almost all came in as spotlight hogs, every year just as brilliant as the year before. Then, slowly we begin to diverge. The actors who endured, and went on to success were the ones who loved the craft. You could see them obsessing over inflections, beat changes and motivations. They would dissect the characters and make them come alive, and fall in love every night on stage. Then, there were the ones like me. I cared more about my face getting seen, and my professors could tell. Vanity, not a true love for the craft was my deeper motivation. I found myself half-stepping my monologues, failing miserably at my auditions, and being combative with my professors for purely egoic purposes. This behavioral pattern initiated a string of events that landed me in the actor's purgatory of theatre tech.

Nothing gets under an actor's skin like longing for the stage and not being able to perform. It's crippling, and leads to some pretty anti-social behavior. Knowing this, they picked the man I would apprentice, and they certainly chose wisely. The dean and professors at the FAMU Essential Theatre put me directly under the tutelage of Mr. Carey Robinson, the master tech of the FAMU stage. A shorter, skinny Black man in his 40's, it was easy to underestimate him. His glasses hid eyes that could assess you with astonishing speed. His wit was stinging, yet benevolent. He was as impeccable as a theater stage had to be, and I would learn the discipline necessary to make a show happen flawlessly. I hung lights, and daisy chained speakers. I built and struck sets, getting splinters in my palms and hair on my chest. By the time Mr. Robinson was done with me, I could do it all. I designed, lit, and built the set for our production of "Mufaro's Beautiful Daughters," and asked for not a word of praise. The set spoke for itself. This brought a sense of satisfaction that is hard to put in words. When your work precedes you, when your craftsmanship speaks, the chest-pounding loses its appeal. Then, something happened; doors began to reopen. This was just when I began to long for the actual craft and process of acting again, not just the spotlight and glory. Slowly I began to evolve into a true performing artist, and I didn't get the outer results I wanted until I changed my inner motivation.

Why are you taking action in the first place? Have you examined the deepest parts of your desire? Are you starting the business because you want to the title of being a millionaire, or do you think your product can truly revolutionize the market? When the going gets tough, which vision will pull you through? Is your passion rooted in a desire to be worshipped, or a desire to serve? In dating, are you hitting the night club because you just want to dance and have fun, or are you secretly hoping to meet someone? When they don't show up week after week, will you be fine with that, or start to feel hopeless? If you hook up for one night with a beautiful stranger, are you chasing pleasure, or chasing commitment and simply afraid to say it? It would serve you well if you knew beforehand.

So the question is, "What keeps our true motivations hidden?" Why do we have this veil covering up the inner workings of our mind? Our brains are full of static. It seems we have all this metal chatter, and don't know which voices are real. This runaway thinking is called the "monkey mind" in Buddhism. Like small chatty primates, our internal noise can be as distracting as it is mischievous, even devious. Picture you are driving in the car with a bunch of baby chimps. Picture none of them in their seatbelts, and their climbing on you as you drive. Now, imagine these monkeys are invisible, and a cop pulls you over. No matter what happens to you or the car, the monkeys won't be held responsible. Only the driver incurs the consequences. The driver is your true self, and you must be able to distinguish who that is at all times. Once you can do that, you can get to putting these apes in their place and back into their seat belts.

This is the emotional intelligence portion of the teaching, and there are no shortcuts to inner knowledge. Shakespeare said, "To thine own self be true, and thou cannot be false to another man." Truer words have never been spoken. So often, we end up deceiving other people when it was ourselves who were not clear on the outcomes we most deeply desired. Look at all we put at stake when we do that. There have been whole marriages swallowed by unacknowledged agreements. These issues pour into the lives of the children involved, the grandparents, the lawyers, and the community, all because we didn't know which monkey was driving our lives...off a cliff.

Instead of real monkeys, let's just acknowledge these monkeys to be what they are; acquired identities. When a baby is born, for the most part their awareness is open to be conditioned by their environment. Humans are so much more vulnerable than other animals because of how long we are helpless to the will of the adults around us. Before we know our name, our race, our religion, our history, the wealth of our families, or the language we will speak, we are just the light of awareness. As we grow, identities are layered over this light like veils of colored cloth over a lamp. Our parents are basically gods at that point. Their teachings sow seeds into our minds like unprotected soil. By the time a toddler is three years old, their grasp on their parent's language is pretty firm. Think about the power of language. These symbols are not just sounds and images, they are data points to our paradigms. These paradigms are more than a network of vantage points, but emotionally charged ideas that our caregivers have accepted as reality. If there is mental poison, limitation, poverty consciousness, unchecked aggression, it shows up in these little bundles of light. It's amazing how many veils we can drape our children's light in, and how short of a time it takes to do it.

What happens when these identities contradict one another? Too often, a child is told that she is free to play, but not to dream of her possibilities. 'I mean, after all, nobody in this family has ever walked in space.' Or perhaps a boy realizes that his love is unconditional, as long as his grades meet the approval of his father, and if they don't, he is outcasted from his father's affections. What reward do we seek for our happiness? What behavior will be reinforced? Does that align with anything the child actually wants for their own fulfillment?

Now, what happens when legitimate trauma occurs, stunting emotional growth? When I taught middle school in the inner cities of Denver, I was surprised at how many adults I knew behaved like the children from 6th to 8th grade. There were times when I could see the kids as little versions of the adults I knew. Then I realized that this age-group was a trauma factory. Middle school is unbelievably rough. Adult hormones and a child-like mind in one body is a lethal combination. These kids were positively wicked to each other. Watching the name calling, the cursing, the bullying astounded me. Intervening was exhausting. These kids were good; good at abuse, that is. By that age, they had often been apt pupils of their parents' dysfunction. Those who did not learn at home learned from each other with chilling efficiency. These wounds often stunt our emotional growth into adulthood, and shape the people we will become. There are 45-year-old people walking around with an 11-year-old making their decisions from within. Being a grown-up, these decisions have far reaching consequences.

Working with these youths made me remember vividly my middle school years. Sure enough, I had picked up some toxic ideas about myself that absolutely followed me into adulthood from those adolescent playgrounds. It was only my commitment to personal growth and life-long learning that gave me the slightest edge in uprooting these mental weeds. This commitment was forged in household where I had two parents that were avid about setting me up for success. Those without the guidance and inward insight that I had were not as fortunate. Throughout my adulthood I would run into those kids who I had first met in middle school and see how many of their paths diverged from mine. Some of these kids were jerks to me, others were my friends. Being fully grown, the fog of childhood worn off, it was clear that only by happenstance did I have the conditions necessary to succeed. My parents nearly forced my sister and I into a high level of emotional intelligence, which drastically changed our outcomes. As they say, there but by the grace of God go I.

Look at what we lose without introspection. Without cultivating the habit for looking internally, we are truly lost indeed. Not only do we become blind to our own motivations, but cause reactions of blindness in people around us. This shows up vividly in relationships. From the time we are children, cartoons, television, video games and even our own parents are forming our ideas about the rights and wrongs in relationships. Whatever the culture values the most, we tend to absorb without observation. I grew up in what seemed to be the golden age of Disney romances. My childhood is filled with memories of my sister and I watching these movies on the big screen. From the Little Mermaid, to Aladdin, Beauty and the Beast and The Lion King, we watched these all as kids unaware of how these movies were shaping our ideas of love. Looking again at these movies with a grown up critical eye, it's no wonder why people end up unrealistic expectations of what love should be.

I noticed that the average age of Disney princesses was around 16, and they were expected to get married. Without going into the legal complications, this would be disastrous in most cases. These ideas of a white knight, a prince to come and rescue women have set problematic relationship expectations for decades. Not to say that standards shouldn't be high, because high enough standards weed out unnecessary drama. However, when the culture does not support these standards, we run into issues. How can a woman be both a woman with carnal needs and a princess on a pedestal? What happens when the need to meet both urges shout within the same body simultaneously? What happened when the man she needs and the man she was taught to go after are not the same guy? The answers to these questions play out in divorce courts across the country in record numbers. We have to be honest with ourselves.

Moving into the correct emotional space to take action can be most of the battle. Fear itself can drive us to destructive action, or paralyze us altogether. Growing up, fear was a constant companion. It stalked my steps in the hallway and traced the vapor around my words. Being a short, skinny, and odd looking kid was a recipe for being targeted in the halls of middle and elementary school. My father being of Caribbean heritage made him pretty staunch about how I dressed. In the islands, and in the West Indian New York neighborhoods he grew up in, dressing clean and neat was a sign of good culture, a mark of coming from a good home. In the 90's, things had changed a little. Sadly for me, Dad missed the memo. I was a walking target every day of my life, it seemed. Gangsta culture dominated my schoolyards, and the kids around me. This combination of factors had me hungry for one thing only: respect. It was an all-consuming obsession. The quest for respect, to climb from my rung at the bottom of the totem pole landed me in more fights than I can count. I then became known as the nerdy dude with fast hands. Bully after bully found out that he could quickly lose his status if he decided to make a go at me.

This quest for respect became a habit, sinking into the background noise of my adolescent mental chatter. Beneath every motive I believed to be genuine was the drive to create a spectacle. Then finally, it was achieved in an epic brawl against a legendary bully in math class in 8th grade. This individual was a terror throughout all my younger middle school years. From random trippings in the hall, to being beat up in the basketball storage closet, this person had been on a 3-year quest to push myself and many others over the edge. A final incident near the pencil sharpener was all it took. I lost it, and the fight was a blur. All I remember was the person with a visibly bruised jaw, turned over desks, and me being the talk of the school on the way to the principal's office. Kids were sticking their heads out the doors on the way down the hall in astonished glee. I watched my legend growing before my eyes. The tale was being told. How I had slain the giant, and things would never be the same in these halls for me again.

After returning from my suspension, the details of the fight had been blown out of proportion in glorious detail. I had apparently also knocked out a teacher and flung a desk at the bully from across the room, hitting them square in the head. Quietly, I relished in my reputation's redemption, despite the trouble I got in. But then, I remember the talk fading, the rumor mill shifting to the next schoolyard conflict. I started bringing up the fight, inserting myself into conversations that had nothing to do with my conflict. At first these interruptions were entertained, soon they became annoying. What had I really wanted in all this fighting? Maybe for that fleeting moment when I was the heavyweight champion of Place Middle School, respect was not the goal at all. Perhaps it was peace. Perhaps it was acceptance. Perhaps it was the quest for the feeling I actually belonged somewhere besides stuffed in a locker.

Pain obscured the truth of what I truly desired. It veiled and masked my deepest motivation, buried in a sea of mental chatter and pain-conceived identity. How heavy these identities become over time. Then, slowly, the weight that used to be a burden fades into the background. This does not exempt it from continuing to cause us problems, however. So what happens? We medicate the pain away with whatever vice takes the edge off the best for us. It's the luck of the draw (or un-luck) which path to self-medication we take. Most likely, it will be what you say in your home environment. If your mom used alcohol, and her friends did to, most likely you will also. If it were harder drugs, like in more extreme circumstances, environmental learning will likely instruct you on how to acquire and abuse these substances. Sometimes it's gambling, sometimes it's porn. Whatever it ends up becoming it takes some heavy awareness to bring it under control, and all because we didn't know what was driving us.

I heard Tony Robbins once say that people sacrifice their values to get their needs met. Truer words have scarcely been spoken. Values and needs occupy different portions of the brain. Values are normally held in the prefrontal cortex, or the decision-making part of the brain. This is where we evaluate and plan, daydream and strategize. The prefrontal cortex is what makes humans human. This piece of machinery is what makes up the difference between us and the rest of the animal kingdom. Self-awareness and identity are networked here. If you call yourself a good Christian, a devout Muslim, a faithful wife, or a providing husband, you call yourself these things because of this part of the brain. The issue is that the vast majority of what lives in the prefrontal cortex is what has been acquired from the external world. From the language you speak, to the pin code to your credit card, that all exists in the prefrontal cortex.

The limbic system and reptilian brain are what you are born with. This is a part that virtually all higher organisms share. Here are where what I call, "The Four 'F's' of Survival" exist: fight, flight, feed, and fuck. The limbic system is your hard-wiring, and it can be triggered before your prefrontal cortex even has time to react, judge, or restrict it. Addictions largely activate this part of the brain, and we've struggled as a species as to how to address these issues. Without question, they drive us, and are more powerful than what our conscious control centers would like them to be.

Luckily, there have been some breakthroughs in the fields of behavioral science and addiction research that might prove quite helpful. What we know about addiction has less to do with habit and more to do with one crucial human need: bonding. Whatever leads us to the deepest sense of connection, safety and wholeness is likely going to be the most compulsive element in our lives. Connection is literally what we live for. Since those warm, quiet days floating in the amniotic fluid of our mother's womb, we have most adored what can most likely to return us to that all-encompassing feeling. This has been operating under the radar for the entire span of human history, driving all sorts of aberrant and destructive behavior. However, once we got out of the womb, humans have evolved a very dynamic replacement for the uterus. That replacement is community.

Humans need community like ants need colonies. In fact, it could be said that you don't understand humans outside of a group context. Like ants, we can have individual lives. We can be isolated and studied, but like ants, to understand what humans are truly capable of, you'd need to see us in groups. From the use of language to our greatest technological achievements, most of what makes people awesome relies on greatly on other people. When we suffer connection issues externally, they reflect themselves internally as well. This is what gets our "monkeys" all out of whack in the proverbial car we talked about earlier. These monkeys signify needs, and when they go unmet, they get crazy. Like a pressurized cabin, an equilibrium must be struck so that things stay harmonious inside and out. Damage these connections with other people, these bonds of safety to our surroundings, and what fills the void can be anything. This can be a dangerous thing. To get that feeling again, no mountain is too high to overcome, nor a valley too low. That sounds like the description of addiction, but it's so much more than that.

Now that we've shined light on this, we can better see through the facades of the things that we believe will give us this connection, and better understand out true motivations. Maybe the theatre kid seeks the spotlight because she has felt a sense of wholeness in the roar of the crowd, or in losing herself in another character. Perhaps this knowledge can give her the walk-away power when a casting agent uses this desire to attempt to take advantage of her. Perhaps we can incentivize emotional intelligence training in early childhood education to thwart the middle-school mayhem that damages so many kids. If only people actually knew what they were looking for, they'd take the correct action to achieve a holistic end. This is so important because we cannot take our actions back. This is a universal law.   What we do with our lives imprints on eternity, so we had better know why we are doing it.

6 THE POWER OF COMMITMENT

In the 1998 movie, "The Siege" starring Denzel Washington, America battled the then-imaginary threat of Muslim extremists. This pre 9-11 movie did its best to envision a scenario where America could actually win the War on Terror. In a showdown with the character played by Anette Benning, one of the suicide bombers calmly explains his philosophy to this privileged Western woman. He said, "You Americans believe money is power; commitment is power." I sat there in awe of the truth of that statement, my mouth wide open in shocked recognition.

Right or wrong, suicide bombers commit not just to the bitter end, but *through* the bitter end. So pit-bull like are they in their mission that the fear of death absolutely vaporizes for them. To their enemies, this is just plain scary. What kind of psychological fortitude does it take to go that far for what you believe in? It seems that virtually no American has something they believe in to that level. The very psychology is so foreign to most of us that we can't even imagine the place where it comes from. Is it the mind? Is it the will? Is it the spirit? What makes a person lose all fear of pain, bodily harm, and the pain of death all to inflict harm on both their enemy and themselves?

It would be so easy to chalk it up to hate and religious dogma, but something in us knows that's not really the heart of the matter, here. While most Americans can point the finger at Islamic extremism, we are just afraid to admit that when a person commits with that level of fervor, they are just more powerful than us.

They have access to something even more potent than faith, a thing most Christians are familiar with. The power of their commitment makes them more than a human, but a force of nature at that point. The ideal that they are willing to die for becomes manifest in them. It is an almost god-like power. Right or wrong, when one is equipped with the power of commitment, things change depending on the motive of the wielder. While watching that movie, little did I know I had witnessed a dangerous form of commitment all my life.

I grew up under the shadow of gang culture. The Bloods and Crips loomed larger than life over what should have been my most innocent years. I'd see these guys around the neighborhood, at the store, at the swimming pool, and I recall being somewhat in awe of them. I remember hearing gunshots before I could distinguish them from fireworks, and then the moment when I finally could. Then, the news caught on. There were so many reports about how lethal they were and the need to wage "war" on them. My parents strove to protect me from all of this. We moved out of my old neighborhood, a Blood stronghold, to a supposedly safer side of town. This did not prevent me from being at school with them, so either way I was surrounded.

When I got older, I became familiar with them on a human level. When your friends become the gangs themselves, you gain intimate knowledge. Not surprisingly, the quality of being "gangsta" was highly valued in gangs, especially in the 90's. This quality manifested in some extreme behavior, especially around initiation. Everything about gangs and thug life is commitment-based when you examine it. It's a warrior code, or "G" code if you will. From the ass-whuppins they take to get put on the set, to the loyalty at the price of death for betrayal, it's all commitment. That's what being 'gangsta' adds up to in my observation. When someone calls you a "G," it's likely because you did something dangerous or difficult that took an extreme level of psychological fortitude. You proved beyond a shadow of a doubt that your commitment to action is unwavering, whatever the price. That kind of respect was terribly appealing to me. There was just one thing holding me back from joining, and this was the gangsta that lived in my house; my father.

That statement is not a metaphor. Before leaving for the war in Vietnam, my father was an active gang member in Brooklyn, New York. He is from the era where thugs could actually fight, and guns were a last resort. No matter how intimidating the big homies were, my father was just scarier in every way. He was bigger, meaner, older, and I depended on him for food...so that was that. This was ultimately a good thing, because in my latter youth, even he couldn't keep me away from the streets completely. There were still arrests, fights and run-ins with the cops in my future, regardless of his efforts. For the most part, however, his presence staved off the damage that could have been done. Inside the walls of my house, my father was teaching me a different lesson on the power of commitment that the gangs were. This was the power of the commitment to keep our family together. At the time of writing this, my parents have been married for 34 years. As romantic as this society would like to paint this picture, at times it was anything but.

My parents were an odd pair. Dad, a gangsta turned veteran, turned electric engineer. My mother is from Los Angeles, and is the eldest daughter of a man that could be conservatively called, "a rolling stone." My grandfather fathered numerous children in the eight marriages of his lifetime. This means that my mother came from a slightly less than consistent home environment. Mom became a 60's flower child and part-time fashion model turned corporate girl. She moved to Denver to follow a job opening with the telephone company. They met at a party, and shortly thereafter my sister and I came along. Despite their vastly different life paths, my parents loved each other dearly, and I could see it. This love would be tested by forces both inside and outside the marriage. From my father being laid off, to my mother's former spending habits, the arrival of my ailing great grandmother, to my father's war PTSD, there was pressure. Yet and still, they worked and built. Because of their commitment, they both were weary never to cross some un-crossable lines. They each learned from previous marriages that some things, you only need do once and all is lost, so they simply didn't do them.

Both of my parents had certain exit points that they could have called their marriage quits. Both had demons to battle. Both are attractive, and could have found other mates to chase what they might perceive as happier lives with. At the end of the day, the reason why they didn't quit...is simply because they didn't. The power of their decision making decided that sticking around was the thing to do, and I thank them for it.

Without commitment, nothing of worth can be accomplished. The power to continue whether one "feels like it or not" is a power that guarantees success. Think about it. This society loves guarantees. Whether it's a money back guarantee or insurance on a car, we seek this type of security in an uncertain world. We'd love this type of guarantee with success, yet it will never come from an outside source. It's all from within. From within is where we decide literally whether we will fail or succeed, and no place else. That which is committed to, gets accomplished. Either you did or you didn't. "Trying" is just a back exit out of leaving no stone unturned and going the extra mile.

One place in my life this was brought to bear was my journey as a vocalist. Singing was something that came naturally to me as a kid, but when puberty dropped my voice through the floor, relearning my instrument was a task. Desire alone was not enough to revive what adolescence had suffocated. I failed horrifically in one attempt after the next. The nuances of these new, bass-heavy vocal chords were extremely difficult to master. I wanted to give up, but the music inside would not quit. Giving that music a voice again would take greater commitment than I imagined. Being a classically trained concert pianist most of my life, I knew music quite well. Tone and pitch were not a problem to hear, but getting this voice to match them was. I needed a vocal instructor. She came to me when I least expected it.

Her name was Sheryl. She was a local jazz legend, singing in a music review at the Denver Civic Theatre. I worked in the coffee shop in the theatre, and would sneak into the balcony seats to watch her during the performances. Frankly, I thought she was sexy in that older, mature way. She was a curvaceous sista with a perfect ebony complexion in her mid-40's at the time, and had a decidedly different appeal from the women in my 20-something age group. Sheryl could have been directly from West Africa, her phenotype betrayed no European admixture, whatsoever. Her profile bordered perfect, a dainty nose, full lips, and big expressive eyes. Physically, she had all the makings of a true Diva with the voice to match. Her deep alto could bottom out near the tenor range, with an almost chopping vibrato and perfect pitch.

She and I both had deeper than average voices for our respective genders. This is when the lightbulb clicked on. She was the one to teach me how to play my new instrument. Working up the courage to talk to her was something else. Luckily, I didn't have to. I ran into her in a night club a few months later, expressing my admiration. Since I had been drinking, this was not a difficult thing to do. She said that she remembered me from the theatre, which was a little more than flattering. I asked her if she taught. She said yes, but never had a male student. I said there's a first time for everything. We laughed and agreed on a price. The journey began.

To say the least, Sheryl could be a harsh master at times. Her critiques cut me deeper than I let on. My flatness, pitchiness, and lack of support were the most constant points of critique. Quietly, I grew insecure to the point of wanting to call it quits. But, looking at the path music lead me down thus far, turning back was not an option. The stars in my eyes over Sheryl went cold, and sobriety hit in the form of the work I had to do. What made me think learning to sing would be less difficult than learning any other instrument? Was this ability not a skill like any other? Developing this was going to be something that took time and dedication, and there was no way around it.

Sheryl eventually moved away, and I was left to my own devices to learn my voice. I remember a string of failed musical theatre auditions, botched community performances, and embarrassing nights at Karaoke. These hurt in a special way because I was so used to wowing crowds with poetry and acting. Singing is a decidedly vulnerable act, and takes some extra courage. Of all the performing arts, the ability to make music come out of one's own body seems to mystify the audience more than any other. It grants an almost immediate star quality to any who can do it well. That this ability eluded me, yet came easily to others was a source of sorrow.

Then, I found my song. It was George Benson's, "Give Me the Night." Upbeat, funky, familiar, and perfectly in my range, it was the perfect choice for almost any setting. Performing this song was the first time, I actually *wowed* a crowd with my voice. It was more than a polite tolerance, but a leaning-in get 'em going feel from the crowds. Black, White, Latino and Asian all got into the music. Their response was secondary to the musical awareness it gave me. I began to actually hear myself, aim and fire at the notes accurately, and gain control of the instrument in my neck. This awareness happily carried over to other songs. Soul music was my go-to, as my gritty texture lent itself to the music naturally. The auditions turned to bookings in musical theatre. My vocal range grew to where I was singing front in cover bands and soon, my YouTube channel would fill up with videos of me confidently covering incredible music. Money followed these opportunities in quantities I didn't think possible, and all because of my commitment to learning a new skill. There's truly nothing like when commitment pays off.

In his seminal book, "Jeet Kune Do," Bruce Lee said that the most dangerous man to fight is the one willing to die trying to rip your eye out. Without skill or training, that man is still the most deadly opponent. He is the one who is most *committed* to the objective, and that is virtually unbeatable. If the greatest fighter who ever lived understood that, we most certainly should take heed. Bruce knew that there is a certain animal power in that kind of ferocity. It takes the fight into a place of pure and unadulterated will. This is the killer instinct so many talk about in the fight world. It's labeled as an instinct because it's the thing you cannot teach. It comes from someplace deeper than the mind; it comes from the very being itself.

So many spiritual systems are missing this key component in the development of their adherents. In fact, it seems as if modern New-Age philosophy seeks to directly remove the difficulty factor out of the equation. It's as if they don't want to drive off customers with any talk of struggle. This seems to be the main thing that separates the teachings of the modern world from the ancient world. I suspect that since convenience has made us considerably softer than we used to be, you can actually sell a spiritual philosophy without a component to deal with challenges, and leave out the spiritual benefit to overcoming them.

The power of commitment was well known to the Yaqui Indians in Mexico, according to Carlos Casteneda. I found his book series while working in St. Louis as a starving actor and part time theatre stage hand. I remember sleeping in a storage closet turned bedroom in a house that clearly justified my $135 portion of rent. I was adrift spiritually having abandoned the church, dabbled in African traditionalism, but never found anything that made sense of my inner world in that way. At the suggestion of my old college roommate, Jay English, I picked up "Journey to Ixthlan." Through that drafty winter, I read how the Yaqui, a branch of the Toltec warrior tradition used difficulty to perfect their action through the practice of "impeccability."

Impeccability was a total commitment to only the action at hand, doing it to the best of one's humanly possible ability, and doing until it was done. I ate this doctrine up, fascinated by how the Yaqui developed this practice under the blade of the Spanish. Their lives in constant danger, they developed a way of committing to every action like it was the last thing they would ever do. In so doing, their being was purified of undesirable qualities such as laziness and procrastination: there simply was no time to indulge in them. While reading that book, every stage I built, every light I hung, every line I learned took me to new levels of excellence and growth. The actual work became its own reward, and that was sufficient since I had to make sense of getting paid $200 a week. Even with this low salary, I saved up and bought a car because I pinched my pennies to that degree.

This brand of spirituality did not put my salvation in some external deity to pray to, no after-death reward. This was a warrior's spirituality, putting faith in one's internal resources, and developing them into a god-like capacity. I contrasted this to what I had been taught in church, which I still attended sporadically. These St. Louis chapels had choirs on par with anything I had ever heard in the south. The preaching caused the emotions to soar and tears to flow. The sense of community was as palpable as the fried chicken was delicious, but still somehow hollow. The actual changing of my soul was coming from how I was living my earthly life, not the hope, belief or prayer for my eternal one.

In church, they often say that faith without works is dead. What is not often discussed is how all aspects of our life comes from that very work. If there is eternal life, after life, or reincarnation, it's all depending on how I live this one, anyway. In that way, this brand of commitment-to-the-now spirituality was far more liberating than any other I had been a part of. There was no fear of demons, no hope for angels. No dreams of seeing my deity's face or fetishizing of his name. The 'here and now' was spiritual enough, and I was to give my all to it. Every drop of sweat was my own holy water because it baptized a life already being well-lived. If there was a God, my belief didn't affect him. If there was no God, my belief would be self-deception. Either way, I was alive. Life was the only thing that I was certain was a miracle. So, I was young, and fiery and fully committed to perfecting the life that I had been given.

Shortly I realized that impeccable action had its own momentum. Being intentionally so good for so long made me accidentally good at other things. Perhaps it was the level of focus I developed, but I know that this fully committed action had carried-over to other areas of my life. I was writing poetry with full emersion into my craft, and performing it with the same intensity. Hell, even sex seemed to brighten in color and heighten in deliciousness. But what was more, I could get a sense of when other people were not fully committed to their actions and how it was totally effecting their lives. When they were sloppy with their workmanship, when they were kidding themselves about the outcomes they wanted, I could see it. It was at first a painful thing to witness, but slowly I grew compassion. There would be times when advice was appropriate, and others when it wasn't but either way, the answers were simple. How much they had or hadn't given to the project of their desire was commiserate with how much they were giving to the rest of their lives.

Commitment in action is one of those things there is no shortcut around. No magic bullet will make you impeccable in any area of your life. The only way to do it is to begin practicing total absorption in all that you do. Commitment doesn't feel like a willed act when you *want* to do it. The key is developing the habit. Once you do, you'll wonder why they don't teach this stuff in schools. If only we told our kids that their dreams were as close or as near as their power to see them through. What if we taught that the difficulties along the way were like teeth on sandpaper whittling their souls closer to perfection? I'm not sure if that would take a massive reformation or education, or just one damn good teacher. What I do know is that I wish I would have learned it earlier. As a kid with head full of inventions and crazy ideas, it would have been great not to have been allowed to quit before competition. To have built the practice of seeing them all through to the end as a child would have drastically changed my destiny as an adult. I imagine the feeling of accomplishment and confidence would have been all consuming, and set me on a path to feeling the sense of being master of my fate much sooner than I felt it as a man. Commitment is a power greater than virtually any other known to man. Cultivated in the unseen garden of the being, it's visible fruits are undeniable. Indeed, it is a power that unleashes all the others.

7 ACTIVATING THE RIPPLE EFFECT

At the Denver Art Museum, there is a display of a sand painting made by Buddhists. So impeccable is the mandala, the spiraling shapes, flower designs, and Tibetan writing, you'd hardly believe that is was done in loose sand. The slightest breeze could completely ruin the painting had it not been in a sealed glass case to prevent even the air conditioner from whisking it into nothing. The irony is that the monks create these sand paintings with the purpose of having them blown away. This is how they meditate on impermanence, symbolically. All that we create, all that we seek to be in this world is simply dust in the wind, as the old song says. Nothing in this world is permanent.

Or is it? Certainly, all living things must die. Certainly, all empires must crumble. However, there's a strange paradox at play here. On one hand, everything that our eyes can see and our hands can touch will fade, but on the other hand, everything we do matters...forever. Forms don't last, but consequences do. Just because my great grandmother is no longer alive doesn't mean that there's no evidence of her existence. Every dollar she spent in the 1940's went somewhere and was counted, added to a ledger that set the foundation for the economy in that town for the years to follow. Every calorie she ate fueled a footstep to a house to take care of kids who are alive today. Every lesson she taught, every mile she drove, every word she spoke is registered somewhere in the physical world, though she is no longer in it. This realm of physical matter is like clay that records the minute details of the sculptor's fingerprint. Every single physical form fades with time, yet every action matters forever. There are numerous examples of what some would call, "the butterfly effect." Where a small, unrecorded action somewhere in the backwaters of history grew into a hurricane of events that reshaped the face of history.

Famously, there is the case of the Fine Arts academy of Vienna rejecting an application in 1905. The name on the application read "Adolf Hitler." Hitler moved to Vienna after his mother died and was forced to live in the slums. During his time there, he was exposed to some anti-Semitic rhetoric that he paid attention to due to his own poverty. His application to art school was his ticket out of the slums. The rejection forced him into armed service. There, young Hitler gained the military experience that lent credibility to his leadership skills and rhetoric. The rest, as they say, is history.

This example is outstanding, but there are more practical demonstrations of the law of action being a self-multiplier. A mentor of mine explained that if your car breaks down and you need help, you don't make a sign and stand by the road, you push the damn thing. The very act of pushing the car triggers something in those who are watching. Something visceral reacts in us and compels us to want to help push whether we act on the impulse or not. The very presence of already-in-motion effort attracts the doer in us. It invites us to do the right thing without being fully responsible for the outcome, and that is attractive to most sane people.

A great example is the Standing Rock protests in North Dakota. When the Dakota Access pipeline threatened to plow over sacred indigenous land and threaten water supply, the Indigenous peoples from across the country gathered together and just pushed. From across the Native American world, they came in solidarity. In cars, by bus, even by horseback, solidarity protesters showed up to resist this blatant injustice. They did this under a veritable media blackout, and under the threat of extreme violence from the state actors brought in to protect the pipeline. The army corps of engineers, who were tasked with building the pipeline project, attracted their own supporters, and the clash got bloody.

There was a lot of uncertainty over the outcome, how far the violence would escalate, and who would even care about the protests. They pushed anyway. Soon actors, political candidates, and the mainstream media would start showing up. Hashtags and solidarity protests emerged, flooding the streets in cities across the country. Wave after wave of non-Native American protestors showed up to support the effort to redirect the Dakota access pipeline, and the national spotlight continued to grow. Suddenly, the plight of First Nations peoples and the history of abuse by the powers-that-be was on the top of everyone's conversation again. The fact that the country had never done right by these human beings was blatant, and any illusions of cultural progress since the days that Native genocide was spoken of openly, were quickly eroding. Out of the efforts of a few, many were encouraged into abandoning their own apathy to do the right thing. Then, the construction of the pipeline was ordered to be stopped by the authorities. A group of veterans had decided to march and join sides with the First Nations peoples. A great cry of victory went out over social media. This cry was tempered with caution, due to the incoming Trump administration and the unpredictable nature of those in power. Through this exercise, some very key things were revealed about human nature, both positive and negative. What was sadly missed by most people was the instruction manual created by those who actions laid the blueprint for success. The actions of a few can leave an imprint for the many to follow.

Notice how the physical world is like clay, yielding to consciousness, our actions leaving the most minute details imprinted onto the physical world. These things, of course, may be covered up, but never undone. Just because sand has covered the pyramids in Egypt doesn't mean that they were never built. At the appropriate time, when technology and collective will find it expedient, the works of those namely ancient ancestors of ours will be uncovered for all to see. Just as with the discovery of the Rosetta Stone, the achievement of the past, once deciphered, will influence generations to come. One can only wonder if those in ancient times knew the impact they would have. Their actions, taken in their respective present day moment, were absolutely critical in humans gaining an understanding of who we are today.

Never undervalue the power you've got in this present moment. This present moment is the long dreamed of future our ancestors never got to see, and the long forgotten past our descendants will imagine with wonder. This becomes apparent if you've ever traced your roots. Finding the evidence of those who came before you is like a treasure hunt for long forgotten pieces of yourself. The journeys of those who came before us, the actions that they took, namelessly shaped the modern world.

In my case, I've only seen one picture of my great-grandfather, Theobald Wilson the 1st. It was lying in a scrapbook that my grandfather gathered, and in it was a picture of his father, our namesake. I know that he was Jamaican. I know that circumstances in Jamaica had him contemplate the future of his family. This man, who I never met, made a decision that effects everything in my life, today. He made me an American by leaving Jamaica. With his wife, Elma Jane Selvin, they set out on a journey that would change the fate of our history, and introduce their descendants to a whole new set of circumstances than they would have encountered had they stayed in Jamaica. All I have is that single photo of him. This man, who stared at the same sun, lived 24 hours in each day, laughed, cried, and loved left one surviving picture. But the events he set in motion will far outweigh that photograph. This is the power we have in our hands.

We've all heard about, "The Butterfly Effect." This is the idea that a tiny butterfly could flap its wings in one part of the word and cause a hurricane in another part of the world. Well, its scientific name is, "The Law of Sensitive Dependents upon Initial Conditions." It works with every form of moving matter, including people. For example, many do not know the story about how African American scientist, George Washington Carver, set forth a series of events that saved the lives of 2 billion people. Carver, who at 19 years old was taking a Dairy Sciences class. Carver's professor had a 6-year-old son named Henry Wallace, and allowed Carver to take his son on expeditions, exploring the wonders of botany. Unbeknownst to Carver, young Henry Wallace never forgot what he was taught by Carver, and grew up to be the United States Secretary of Agriculture. So excellent was Wallace's work there, he was tapped by Franklin Delano Roosevelt to be the Vice President. During his time as VP, he created a research station in Mexico whose sole purpose was to hybridize corn and wheat for arid climates. Their theory was that if they could do this, they could create food supplies that could feed people all across the world and do it cheaply with simple replication. In order to do that, they hired a botanical expert, Norman Borlaug. Borlaug succeeded at the task. The result was the successful hybridization of corn and wheat in products that could be shipped around the world, and prove as a stopgap between poverty and starvation for 2 billion people and counting. All of this starting from the actions of a 19-year-old George Washington Carver, mentoring a little boy who would quietly change the world.

This ability for action to compound onto itself is where the law of attraction gets its apparent 'magic.' What people are often unaware of is that the original hermetic axiom was, "Act, and ye shall attract." Action was the original mate to the law of attraction before the modern New Age movement began to teach it as a separate energy. The fact is that as long as you are a part of the physical universe, the law of action is an attraction never stops working. Either you take action, or action takes you. The key to power is in taking action that attracts the response you desire in the first place. How do you act in a way that will compound the effects that you desire and use it for your own ends?

One way that I found was the through the internet. I desired to make viral videos that would get my message out to the world in a way that would make substantial change. I had made a few video posts before, but none of them had the kind of smashing effect I wanted to have. What happened when I discovered a subtle shift in my messaging was profound. Instead of being all content based, I started making videos with a lot of controversy and emotionally charged rhetoric in the first minute of the video. Then, I calculated the reaction and laid out the facts in an order that would slowly calm the storm I had stirred up.

The next step was picking a topic. I had been reading Ta-Nahisis Coates' work on reparations. I decided it was controversial enough to make an impact. My process began with sketching out notes on pieces of paper and compiling my argument. The first minute of the video was me espousing ant-reparations rhetoric in a way that appeared to be my actual opinion. Some viewers didn't make it past the first minute. Others stayed and were so blown away, that they shared. Even with that strategy, it only got so far. With momentum slowing, a friend of mine who was part of a multi-level marketing company messaged me. Her advice was simple; change the damn privacy setting to public and start sharing it in your groups! I obeyed, and the video took off.

Going viral for the first time was a dizzying quantum leap into cyber fame. It is amazing watching the action you take end up taking on a life of its own. Literally overnight, I was a public figure. The comment section was full of praise and critique, profound insight, and outright racism...but it was hot. The video seemed to multiply upon itself exponentially. Two views turned to four, turned to sixteen turned to sixty-four. The friend requests were so abundant that Facebook flipped to my settings to only receive followers without me touching a button. I had hoped to only get 10,000 views. But the time the video was done, it was viewed of over 160,000 times.

That would not be my most successful viral video by a long shot. Soon, Hollywood casting agents who liked my look contacted me and began to ask for my information. Marriage proposals, sexy pictures and death threats became a part of my regular life, and I adjusted accordingly. As my followership grew, so did my responsibility. People were coming to me for answers, and I was expected to know them. This forced me to spend more time researching and understanding, but it was all completely healthy. Being on point with my information is a source of pride and confidence, so in this way, pressure formed a diamond. This commitment to excellence is likely what drew you to this book that you are reading right now.

Act and ye shall attract. This is the secret to the universe. If you are alive, you will be engaging and creating something, intentionally or not. Creating momentum in the physical world is the best way to attract what you want. Once your idea begins to take shape in the physical world, it is literally real. Engage the universe, physically, and the metaphysical things will follow if your consciousness and intentions are aligned. Whether you are internet famous, an activist, an inventor, or an average person, this law never shuts down. Everything we do literally matters for all time. The space time universe has made room for you to be here. You are in some ways an investment of creation. The atoms lent to you will be returned in time, but for the time they belong to you...engage.

8 THE GIFT OF SECOND FORCE

Without gravity, what's the point of a pushup? Without disease, what's the point of your immune system? Without challenges, what's the point of perseverance? Iron sharpens iron, but if iron could feel, the sharpening process would hurt. The losing of one's original self, the whittling away of the unnecessary is the only process for revealing that which is within. In this outcome-based society, we want the finished product, neglecting the process because it's often too hard. Yet, it is in difficulty, in second force, that we find out what we are made of.

The ancient Egyptians understood this well. With their language and paradigm, this civilization came to very profound conclusions about the nature of reality, and how to explain it. They embodied abstract principles of the universe in their deities, and gave them mythologies to explain the mechanics of these principles. Western explorers and interpreters believed archetypes to be "gods" to be worshiped, not concepts to be studied. One of these ancient Egyptian entities was named, Set. He represents the difficulty principle inherent in the physical universe. Set forms the mythological basis for "Satan." Modern Christian understanding labels Satan as "the enemy" whereas Set was "the opponent" in Egyptian understanding. This is a key distinction in understanding the world view of the ancient peoples, and the wisdom inherent in their paradigm. An enemy is malevolently opposed to you with single minded intent to destroy all that you hold dear. An opponent is someone whose opposition to you is there to bring out the hidden greatness within your being. When you see two boxers in the ring with one another, rarely are they trying kill their opponent. The competition is to find out who the best is, but it's ultimately life-affirming.

The Egyptian entity known as Horus, or "Heru" is a metaphor for the human will. Heru is the part of us that decides, and can be identified as our truest essence. Heru and set did battle in the mythology to demonstrate that human will, in action, will encounter difficulty. This difficulty is a healthy thing. If we suffer under a paradigm that says our natural opponent is an "enemy" then we miss the lesson. That which is known as "evil" is often just an unpleasant difficulty to bring out the best in us. This distinction informs the action we take.

Resistance breeds persistence. It is there to be overcome. When we engage the law of action, we must engage it with this principle in mind, or be disheartened upon our journey. So the trick is to embrace the challenge. To love it and welcome it in as a brother. When we do this, our relationship changes to the challenge. We become Heru in our own lives. It's probably a good idea to draw attention to the similarity in the words "Heru" and "Hero." The hero's journey, the story of overcoming obstacles, slaying dragons, rising above temptations, and ultimately triumphing is a hold-over from the original mythos of Heru vs Set, which begat Hercules vs Hades, and is mirrored in Christ vs. Satan. The ancient ones realized that these stories were not about the gods, they were really about you.

Obstacles are built into nature herself. The things that keep us from expanding are gifts that cause us to reach beyond our limitations. Through the fires, the difficulties, we begin to get in touch with the inner powers that make us soar when we apply them. If these challenges are especially steep, some of us are tempted to give up all together, and some even wish to cease living. Yet, these are the very difficulties that great stories are made of; this is how legends are born. We like watching movies and hearing stories where a heroic spirit pushes beyond enemies and pitfalls that we feel would have ended us. Thus, the power of perseverance becomes a most attractive quality in people. It inspires us to go even further than we could have gone without that example. In leaders, we look for it. In a spouse, it's indispensable. Without the difficulty principle, without necessary second-force, it cannot be developed.

Knowing that second-force is going to be in the equation no matter what, we can calculate it and move accordingly. Developing a strategy with resistance in mind is never a bad move when planning to take action. Therefore, one of the best moves to make in an action plan is to minimize second force by not letting on what you're about to do; the element of surprise. We know that this works in street fights. More often than not, he who hits first, hardest, and most often is likely gonna be the winner. In boxing, trainers drill fighters not to "telegraph" their punches because it elicits the second-force in the other boxer to react, and thwart the plan to victory. So, we must sometime apply this principle in our own lives.

You must be wise enough to know who you can and cannot share your plans with. Some people are dream killers. To tell them your own dream will only cause them to tell you why you'll fail. When these people are in one's own family, or in the same house, it is often difficult to contain one's excitement. Yet and still, you must consider second force. The energy you spend debating your merits with them could best be spent on actually making your dream a reality. Why spin your wheels with ignorant people? It's just going to be one more negative voice to get out of your head when you are in motion. That would make you the ultimate cause of the second force in your way. In this case, wisdom would dictate that silence is the best course of action; non-action.

Here's a true story about minimizing second force before a major life change. There was once an ex-soldier living in Harlem who had more than his fill of New York. He had done it all; from running the streets to running a small enterprise, from playing the numbers, to playing with women's hearts, his joy had run its course. With a failing marriage, PTSD, and a wicked case street karma on his heels, he knew a move was imminent. The late 1970's were a violent time in the big apple. The city seemed hell-bent on consuming the lives of those who could not find a way to become bullet proof. Though he could not fortify his body, he found a way to safeguard his mind. After encountering the works of Gurdjieff, he found a moral compass that lead straight to within. When he went within, the voice said leave. He had to obey, but how?

Fortunately, during his time as an enlisted man, he had been stationed out west and found a town that he saw himself living in. It was big enough to be a city, yet small enough to still see the stars at night unblocked by looming steel towers. He contacted a friend out there, and warned them to keep the secret. He was on his way west. The leaving process was quiet. Slowly he sold what he could not fit in his Camaro. Without telling family and friends, we turned his belongings into the cash he would need along the way. Then two weeks before the exit, his father stopped by for a surprise visit, as he had not heard from his son in a while. He found his son's apartment almost empty. Upon his father demanding an explanation, he informed him of the imminent departure. Talking him out of it was an exercise in futility seeing that nearly all his belongings were gone anyway. Since the divorce from his wife was a mere legal formality at this point, there was no reason to stay. The momentum of his action had gone too far to look back, and he liked it like that. His exodus assured by the power of his sovereign heart, he packed his car and looked at the skyline. New York rained in sheets that night. It was as if the city was crying as her favorite son was turning his back on it forever. Like a lover with his backed turned in the doorway, he kissed the windshield and fired up the Camaro. The adventure had just begun.

He stopped through city after city, being present and taking pictures. His new life raced toward him with every highway sign, every white stripe on the interstate, every cloud formation he drove by. There was freedom in action. It was him, the wind, the road, and his decision. Without a city full of people clinging to him, his exit was triumphant as the day he was born.

Without him this very book would not exist, for this ex-soldier is my father. Private First Class Sidney T. Wilson was stationed in Colorado Springs before his return to New York, and took a road trip up to Denver. When he returned to the mile-high city, it was not long before he met my mother, and my story would soon begin.

The trials that my father endured revealed what was within him, as the trials that you endure expose your true character. Character is a word that used to mean something in this society. Personality gets all the praise these days, yet character is the foundation. The word literally means, *"the aggregate of features and traits that form the indivi dual nature of some person or thing." In other words, what you are made of. Character is who you are, whereas personality is a social adaptation. If people around you were aggressive, you may have adapted the behavior to survive, and so forth. Character, however, is only revealed at a crossroads situation. Character is the choice you make when no one is looking, and that choice involves action, often.*

What makes a strong character is difficulty. Dilemmas and uncertainty cause us to go within and ask the hard questions. When we do that, we unearth the jewels hidden inside of us because there is no place else to go for this treasure. In some respects, one should pray for a difficult life circumstance just as a bodybuilder seeks heavier weight. Some of us have muscle-bound souls, and it shows up in our lives. Sometimes, the only way to gain mass in this area is raw sacrifice. We must be forged in the fires of difficulty if we are to come out swords of any caliber.

An old Yaqui Indian tale speaks of the value of difficulty. In Carlos Castaneda's book, The Fire from Within, his master talks of the value of tyrants as spiritual teachers. An insufferable tyrant teaches the student to lose their self-important sense of ego and a sense of patience, or forbearance. Forbearance was not patience for patience's sake, but patience for the purpose of allowing the universe to show you the right moment to strike, and to not suffer while waiting.

There is a spiritual way to orient oneself toward difficulty and second-force that creates joy within the disciple. I have seen this in brothers who go to prison. They prepare themselves mentally by looking for the positives in what is universally known as a negative difficult event. They begin to look forward to three meals a day, the guys they know already in there, and the street respect they'll get for doing their bid. This becomes a rite of passage for some, and though there can be negative effects, the wisdom in taking this mindset is clear. If you learn to embrace the hard times, too, you become emotionally invincible. There is nothing that can harm you because you will not allow it, and that is a gift only second force can give.

I saw this in full effect when I worked as a youth corrections officer in Watkins, Colorado. The name of the program was called, "Rites of Passage," and it was indeed aptly named for that period in my life. I was learning to master second force while being trained in Kupigana Ngumi. Dr. Meeks, taught us to embrace any challenge that came our way to cultivate a warrior spirit. Having been unemployed for months, the opportunity to work at the facility was a challenge I couldn't afford not to take.

The program was special because of the rigorous physical demands they placed upon the youth incarcerated there. There were 18/20 and 18/30 military drills almost daily. These consisted of eighteen exercises like crunches, pushups, and burpees to completed for twenty to thirty reps each. On days when they did not exercise, they were to subject to mandatory, site-wide three mile runs, which had to be completed in twenty four minutes or less. They had this curriculum to burn off the excess testosterone festering in their loins, and rehabilitate them from a life of drugged-out slacker-ism. As a staff member, I had the option to back out of the labor. Dr. Meeks would not approve of such cowardice, so I dove headlong in.

Being a former high school sprinter, I had never run more than a half a mile without stopping. Even these drills made my lungs swell up with mucus and burn like I inhaled an ant colony. Running three miles was like asking me to run the rings of Saturn without a space suit; laughably impossible in my mind. However, seeing boys that were former meth addicts and cokeheads ace these runs challenged my manly pride in an uncanny way. I knew full well that when it came to real world fighting, endurance is the most underestimated weapon. If I got into a physical management conflict with one of these boys, I risked being epically embarrassed. My only way through was to embrace the challenge.

Of the boys in the entire facility, one stood out among them all. Staff called him "Mr. Invincible." No punishment scared him. No exercise phased him. Physical exercise was used as a punishment, and he learned to welcome the exhaustion. For the sake of this book, we will call him Dontrell, and he was a living legend at Rites of Passage program. He chewed up and spat out 18/30 drills like bubble gum. He ran 3 miles at suicide speed, hoping his heart would stop, and one day it almost did. Dontrell was short, black, wielded a wiry muscular frame, and a defiant attitude to the core. He scared other kids, pissed off the staff, but I was in awe of the kid. Quietly, he reversed the leadership roles when it was time for physical training. Before I knew it, I adopted his mentality and pushed my body to limits that it had never known. I went from stopping and jogging in our runs to fully leading them, darting out ahead of the boys and setting the pace.

Then, I realized the true nature of any initiation, of any true rite of passage. It is finding a task you are nowhere near strong enough to accomplish, and then becoming the person who can. It is to walk the path of a butterfly, and hatch into something you never thought you could be. It will be hard: embrace the difficulty. The resistance is a gift. Wrap it like a cocoon around you and let it incubate your wings. The ancient Egyptians said that all of life is in initiation, a rite of passage. These challenges we face are meant to be overcome, to be unlocked like a riddle, and conquered. The ancient ones set up the mystery schools as accelerated courses to unlock human potential. These mystery schools had very steep challenges, sometimes fatal. However, they were walked through these difficulties with the wisdom of master-teachers at their side, and this journey would cultivate a super-being.

Perhaps some of your life is fraught in difficulty. A challenge may be the fact that you are without a master-teacher to cultivate within you the wisdom necessary to not suffer needlessly through the gauntlet. Without consistent external guidance, one must adopt a healthy perspective. The right angle on a situation can indeed make all the difference in the world. Understand that second-force, negativity, and difficulty is built into every situation. Any expansion that you wish to undertake, you must factor in the opposition. Some strategies may involve avoidance and minimization;

others may involve direct confrontation. Either way, once you've embraced the challenge, you will be equal to the task.

9 THE ART OF ALLOWING

The universe is never standing still. Something is always being done. The Earth is always spinning, and hurtling through space at 67,000 miles per hour. You may be sleeping, but your heart is beating, and food is being metabolized. Water is evaporating, plants are growing, and the flow of human events is an endless river of action and reaction. There is action going on, literally all of the time. This is precisely why if you don't take action, action takes you. Nothing really ever stands still, and it's a good thing. We are part of a never-ending stream of events that are far bigger than we are, and in a way, it all has a life of its own.

Earlier, we talked about the tendency of the universe to be cruel and amoral. We discussed how violence, death, chaos and decay seem to be woven into the very fabric of existence itself. These less friendly traits of the universe are more widely recognized as the "true" nature of life. Scientists, naturalists, and atheists point out the vast coldness of space, the brutal predation of nature, and the utter aloneness of planet earth to make the point that we are ultimately an orphaned and godless species. At first glance, they certainly have more than valid points. Certainly, there are violent and destructive forces in the universe, but unlike many violent humans, universal violence serves a purpose. That purpose is balance. That purpose is to strike a dynamic, living equilibrium, and once that extreme violence accomplishes this end, beautiful things begin to happen.

Of course, the coldly intellectual cynic types shy away from another aspect of the universe; the benevolent interpretation. The universe is cold and dark, yet it is peppered with the warmest, hottest of suns, galaxies and nebula. These star systems seem to have a vast and predictable order about them, and this order replicates on the same patterns throughout the observable universe. These patterns signify that where stars and matter are involved, the universe tends toward order. Surely, the vastness of space seems to be a chaotic wasteland, but where stars are involved, and there are trillions of them, rhythm and pattern begin to happen. Familiar shapes like spheres and spirals begin to occur. Fractal geometry arises. Gravity begins to create orbits in celestial bodies that are no different from the ones in our very solar system. The laws of nature seem to become predictable again.

And now, we have evidence that something else is happening. It turns out the Earth, a "Goldie Locks" habitable-zone planet, is far from unique. NASA's Kepler program began to find other planets with atmospheric conditions like our own. These planets were in the habitable zones of stars that would make them fertile ground for life. In fact, Kepler observed a possible 40 billion earth sized planets in the habitable zones of stars in the Milky Way, 11 billion of them in solar systems with stars the size of our sun. Perhaps the vast darkness is also a condition for life. Maybe all that emptiness is to give the stars enough room on the dancefloor to boogie, the icy coldness to balance out the heat of the suns so life forms can find equilibrium. If this is the case, the entire universe could be in the life-making business.

From another angle on the same data points that say the universe is cold and unfeeling, one could say that it is benevolent. Our bodies cannot survive the vacuum of space, yet the elements that form life came from nowhere else than this vacuum. Every rain drop, every molecule that plants consume, every insect, dinosaur, mouse and mammoth was made from a particle that was once floating in "nothingness." Then, these molecules, with an alarming tendency towards order, arranged themselves into staggeringly symmetrical, self-aware macro-life forms in a relatively short period, evolutionarily speaking. Are we to believe that this happened against the will of the mighty universe a possible 40 billion times in our galaxy alone?

The scientific community, with all its claims to objectivity, seems shun the evidence contrary to a chaotic, uncaring universe. I suppose it lingers dangerously close to "intelligent design" and a suggestion that the architecture of the universe must have had...an architect. These cerebral, objective scientists can get quite emotional rejecting the notion of intention and order in the universe. Their blind fear of looking like they have faith in anything besides what is observable is reminiscent of a trauma survivor. It's as if organized religion is the estranged, abusive dad they reject any conversation about. Some scientists argue that the natural forces of the universe want them dead, forgetting the natural forces that gave the oxygen to make the argument. They don't seem to want to be told of their resemblance to anything religious, but their rejection is telling. Behind the claims of objectivity seem to be the all-too-human traits of emotionally driven bias toward a specific world view. Yet, the data is the data, and we must take it into consideration.

Something in this universe is pro-you. You need not stoke, prod or trigger it, it is huge and operating always for you. In fact, you are too small and insignificant for it not to be in your favor. If it wanted you dead, it would have killed us all by now and not even have batted the proverbial eye. Therefore, it is only logical that whatever these forces are that enabled your life out of the cold blackness of space is still working for you. It operates not only in the vastness of space, but in the realm of human events right here on Earth. All of us are in the flow.

It was a revolutionary concept to me when I first considered that the universe was conspiring in my favor. I was in the depths of my warrior training under Dr. Meeks when I found a book by Paulo Coelho entitled, "Warrior of The Light." It was a simple series of mazing uplifting quotes that helped me through the rigors of my training and initiation. One of the quotes in there stated, "We warriors of the light must be prepared to have patience in difficult times and to know the universe is conspiring in our favor, even though we may not understand how." That was profound to me. I could see the sun, moon and stars in a ballet of assistance in my existence. A supernova happened some eons ago to make the stardust in my knuckles every time I threw a punch. The people I meet, even the ones who dislike me, all playing their part in the opera of my life. Interestingly, the Bible also says something similar to this. Romans 8:28 states that, "All things work together for good to them that love God, to them who are called according to His purpose." I am not advocating

Christianity or any religious belief, but to those who are spiritually in-tune, this truth becomes self-evident when looking at the data.

When we are born onto this Earth, there is a symphony of circumstances hovering around our parents. These circumstances are directly related to the karmic elements set forth by our parents. If you were not supposed to be born, a myriad of possible things could have occurred to prevent that from happening. Your parents could have coupled a day too early or late. Your mother could have been in an accident, experienced a catastrophic health problem, or decided to terminate the pregnancy. Nine months is a long time for any of these possibilities to unfold, yet they didn't. After your birth, any number of similar hazards could have prevented your growth and survival. If you weren't touched and loved, you'd have died from "failure to thrive" syndrome. You could have been dropped, squished, or neglected. You were physically helpless, and through no power of your own, you are here.

Prisoners used to say, "I don't serve time, I let time serve me." In the real world, this mindset is quite an asset. However, like double-dutch, you've gotta be ready to jump on the opportunity when it arises. Like planting a garden, the botanist can only initiate the process, gather the materials, and set the right conditions. The actual growing is done by the wisdom of the seed within the soil, time, sunlight, and water. The cellular division is not his concern, nor is process that turns chutes to flowers. Time and the programming within the DNA of the plant will take care of the detail work.

Dr. Wayne Dyer spoke of the Power of Intention. This power is not the power of dogged human determination, but rather the patient wisdom governing the form and timing of all manifested things. It is the intention of that which created this universe. He said the power of intention is un-erring. A cabbage seed always grows into a cabbage, never a cherry tree or a radish. The process and timing of the creation of the cabbage is woven into its very shape, size, flavor and season. Growing season is growing season, and harvest time is harvest time. Not a single word of a non-acceptance of the seasons will make the planet spin faster or slower. We simply must trust in the organically assigned unfolding of it all after we initiate the action.

This pattern of unfolding events is represented by a spiral in many cultures. The concept of time in ancient cultures was cyclical, not linear. Like the rings on a tree, each round adds something to the picture, but is yet familiar. This is helpful to remember. When we set in motion a project, the development is often governed by a law that we cannot rush, and often does better at manifesting than we could have initially imagined. When writing this book, I was amazed at how the events of my day would contribute insight into the topic that I was writing on. Once set in motion, the writing process took on its own momentum.

One example of non-action being the path to freedom is the healing process. Some things cannot be rushed. Whether a broken leg, or a broken heart, time does what we cannot. If you you've tried to jump into a new relationship too soon after a break-up, you know what I mean. Not allowing time to re-establish your footing after having your other half ripped away from you can hurt not only yourself, but the new person. What's so deceptive about the healing process after a relationship is the fact that you could be good all by yourself, but still not be ready to love again. How can you tell? There seems to be no easy answer.

A relationship-readiness metaphor that helped me is the one about the canoe. You can be good at paddling all on your own, and have a pretty strong stroke. You may believe that you can afford a little company in your canoe, but can you? Once another person steps in, there will be weight and balance issues, and possible problems with buoyancy. Are you strong enough to paddle with both of your weights, and maintain your equilibrium? This is an assessment you must be able to make, and you must allow yourself the space and time to find out. Nothing about the process can be rushed.

Similarly, a broken bone creates the same challenge. Any athlete knows the trials and difficulties of staying put for the sake of healing when the body wants to get in the game. Yet, too soon putting pressure on an injury, and you may never play again. Indeed, for someone used to an active life style, to sit on the sidelines is a form of hell. It creates fear and agitation about the future of one's participation in the beloved game or activity. Those with martial, yang personalities struggle with this aspect of allowing most of all. But it's quite a healthy developmental challenge. The art of not-doing creates patience, a character trait that I have struggled with mightily. Yet and still, the universe has it's time to do its work, and there is no changing that. Somewhere along the way, we lost trust in the wisdom of it all. Yet, we would be nothing without the miracle.

Consider the growth of a baby. Not just the miracle, but the symmetry of it all. The blastula of cells shortly after conception resembles the flower of life in sacred geometry. Then the cellular mass nearly cleaves itself in two, growing in opposite directions. When the two halves meet again, they connect in the center and the heart is formed. The entire structure looks like a figure eight of infinity at this point. Then, every human life goes through what resembles an accelerated evolution, taking a fish and even reptilian form before resembling something human. Everything must go absolutely right in this process. One single step missed, a single mutation or division out of place, and the baby either dies or is deformed. Are we to suppose that this wisdom only takes place inside the womb? Should we think that there is no other place to witness this perfection?

In the Michael Talbot's "The Holographic Universe," the author talks about the theory of, "The Implicate Order." This is to say that the universe is divided into the physically manifested, and non-manifested world. The implicate order scientifically is referred to as a 'field of quantum potential.' It is a realm of infinite possibilities. This shows up in human awareness as the world of ideas, thoughts and dreams. Technically, these are already "things," fully formed and real. The difference is that they have not broken into the plane of the physical world. Our minds, our consciousness is the only way we contact the implicate order, and when we act upon them, they become manifested. What is often missed is the 'order' part of the 'implicate order.' According to Talbot's research, the way that these ideas, inventions and potentialities unfold is upon an organized template, invisible to the naked eye. For example, oak trees come from acorns, yet when you cut one open, you do not see an oak tree waiting to absorb added water and expand like a sponge. However, it is there. It is "enfolded" into the proteins and DNA of the seed. From its height to the patter of its branches, it is all there in the implicate order hiding in the seed. When it is planted in the ground and watered, the unfolding begins. The un-manifested becomes manifested, and it does so according to its internal implicate design.

The fact is that certain things cannot be rushed once initiated. No amount of willpower, force, or action can expedite the coming forth of certain desired results. Our hearts may be in the correct place, yet our action could ruin the outcome. In some cases, we must learn to trust the process. Indeed, it may prove itself wiser than we are, and the best thing we can do is get out of its way. The trick is to know the difference. When do we act, and when do we fall back? Thought we never may be able to collect enough data, to always make the correct decision, there do seem to be a few indicators.

Firstly, forcing the issue never turned out right for me. My journey has evolved into one of exerting a kind of effortless effort. I am always in touch with my spiritual center. Meditation taught me what it feels like to be emotionally balanced. It feels like I am in touch with my true self when I am in meditation. If the accomplishment of a goal requires me moving entirely too far from this place, it's at the very least a red flag. Either I am doing the wrong thing, or doing the right thing the wrong way. It does not help to lose oneself in this fashion. Namely, this is because at the end of the day, all you've got is yourself. Your wits, your internal resources, and your talents are tools best used in a state of mental and emotional clarity. If the job, the relationship, the project or task is having you spend more time off kilter than you can sustain, it's time to do a checkup on your process. You may be planting out of season. You may be beating a dead horse. It has been entirely true that when I am in the flow of events in the highest way, the effort, though great, has a healthy and expansive feeling to it. When my goal is in harmony with what the rest of the universe seems to want, the correct doors seem to open along the journey.

Always be checking in with the center of your being. This means develop a practice of being in touch with quietude and silence. It means developing a habit of true introspection, healthily questioning the narrative your mind is feeding you about your life and situations you encounter. Is it real, or am I projecting my nonsense onto what I am seeing? If the latter is true, it's time to reevaluate the situation and the action I will take in it. Perhaps it's already being worked out to a conclusion better than you could have intended. If that is the case, don't fix what isn't already broken. Breathe, center and check in with yourself, and see where you fit into the flow of a situation. Haitian-American poet, Carvens Lissaint, once said, "I was one who never spoke unless it improved on silence." Actions speak louder than words, but do they improve on stillness? Develop the clarity and faith to know, and watch your actions gain power, exponentially.

He looked at me again and said, "But, what are you actually giving to your followers?" Jay English was hard to bullshit. Years spent on the Trenton, New Jersey streets left a sharpness to his yoga-guru persona. Jay's profile and eyes were hawk-like, and always reminded me of a black version of Tom Cruise. His thin frame could make you underestimate him physically, almost. I had explained to him that viral video fame had made me quite the center of attention on social media, and the power given to me was balanced out by the graveness of the responsibility. But, what was I contributing to their lives? The answer was not immediately apparent.

This is how his questions challenged me for the decade-and-a-half that I had known him. Jay English, formerly known as the rapper, "Honors English" or "E-clipz" had been my roommate for half my undergrad years. He served as an unwitting mentor, though I was five months his senior. We sat in Japanese fusion restaurant waiting on our order. As the preliminary miso soups and ginger salads came out, English explained to me his energy healing practice. After undergrad, he immersed himself in yoga and meditation. His initial reasons were for purposes of clearing his own mind and seeking higher consciousness. The insights that he found lead him to do this for others, and now he had gained knowledge enough to deserve compensation for his healing abilities...because they genuinely worked. Jay English was changing people's lives in a calculable way. His unique skillset was elevating people, and he could demand a fee for it. The value they got was actually worth far more than what he charged. His contributions were based on his divine gift, and was really the only ethical way to practice capitalism in this society. What could I do to create greater freedom for all those who encounter my gift, including myself? My task and challenge were to figure out a way to do what Jay had done with what I'd been given.

It was turning out to be a sobering conversation with the soberest mind I knew under 35 years of age. In our booth at that restaurant, we began our existential investigation. What did I really have to give? Where would I begin, and in what direction would I start my journey to being a contributor? There was always my poetry, a path that I had taken after spending years listening to Jay and his battle rap crew, 1st Ave, in my undergrad at FAMU. After English literally sat down and taught me the art of the punch line, I had acquired years of rap knowledge in just a few sittings. At times, I'd reflect that the multitudes of people who knew me as Lucifury, the poet, had no idea from whom I had attained such a proficient foundation.

I had sold my albums on couch tours and at universities. After winning the National Poetry Slam in 2011 with Slam Nuba, I had booked touring gigs before I could step off finals stage, trophy still in hand. Once I got on the road, slowly, the Slam scene lost its appeal to me. The cult of personality that I had earned after winning the largest poetry slam in America seemed like a fleeting victory at best. Couch surfing across the country, wrecking poetry venues to sell CD's while hoping to get laid on the road didn't seem like the path to stability. What was clear to me was that my time spent as a competitive poet had developed a high verbal proficiency. This, I told Jay, was the secret to the success of my online videos. My followers loved not only my message, but how I delivered it. A great deal of the topics I would have turned to poems I turned to videos. Jay listened as I told him that whatever it was of value I was bringing to the table, it most certainly revolved around the power of my words.

The main course arrived, and we dug in. Over two gorgeous plates of Japanese cuisine, we narrowed down a solution. I told Jay of my frustration on not being able to get my YouTube channel as popular as my Facebook. Had I been able to do that, I probably could generate some stability for myself outside of the job that I took to stay afloat. Jay laughed and said, "No, no, no. Your fans love what you're saying, you need to write a book." I laughed hard enough to draw attention from neighboring tables. "Oh, yeah. Lemme just up and write a book, cause that's some easy shit, bruh." Jay was amused by my sarcasm, but not moved. Our conversation drifted as we caught up on missed time. Checks came and life went on, so I thought.

That night, laying on Jay's couch trying to go to sleep, my mental wheels could not stop turning about the conversation we had that evening. I stared at the ceiling fan, the only thing that made the Tallahassee summer nights cool enough to sleep through, and remembered what a few of my Facebook followers had said. On several occasions, I remember people asking me to write a book after liking or commenting on thought provoking posts. These posts often involved me debating with "spiritual" people about the merits of the law of attraction and the teachings of "The Secret." My observation was that the teaching absolutely wreaked of Western privilege. The entire doctrine seemed highly incomplete to me. Mere positive thinking and vision boarding could work for someone in America, but what about Uganda? In places on the planet where the people had significant obstacles to their desires manifesting, the law still had to work, or we could not call it a law.

These New-Age philosophies seemed to be lacking some elbow-grease, a real-world and muscly way to deal with difficulty. I remember hearing a sage say, "Act, and ye shall attract." Action always works to kick-start manifestation, and attraction is the byproduct. This is true from Indiana to Indonesia, from Albany to Aleppo. This was the actual secret, to me, and like many of the deepest truths, it was simple. By God, that was it. I was going to write a book about the law of action, and though I had never written a book before, I already had a little practice. For example, when writing a powerful slam poem, I didn't just sit down and construct the poem, I lived it. My very walk in life had to give me the right words, or else the poem would lack connectivity. This is the process I would use to write the book, I just had to find the secret to beginning. How on Earth would I start when inaction seemed to have me by the balls?

Then, a very simple realization hit me; I was going to do something, anyway. Whether that 'something' was fixing myself some food, going to take a dump, or getting back on the airplane from Florida to Denver, unless I died, action would be done. Dammit, that was it. As long as I have a body, I am subject to the laws of physics, and thereby subject to the law of action. I can't not take action. The law never turns off. So as long as I was going to be sucking in air, I'd best complete the task of sitting down to write.

Then I assessed my tool kit. Being a columnist for the Denver Urban Spectrum, I was already familiar with the process of writing editorials. What else was a book but a long-ass editorial? I would have to write each chapter like a series of articles, but it could be done. I knew I had the discipline, but a book would be a long-term commitment, or so I thought.

One of the biggest obstacles I experienced was an internal barrier of epic proportion. My history of failures and false starts all traced back to good ideas that I'd had throughout the years. Self-doubt is a haunting and highly efficient de-motivator when it comes to the completion of any project; this book was no different. I have had so many good ideas that I started, but never finished. If you're anything like me, your action may be the result of a lightbulb moment, but the light that emanates from good ideas and good intent is often dimmed by a short attention span. The Law of Action demands that you fight against the disappointment and avoid self-sabotage at all costs, consciously allowing the universe to propel you to the intended goal. It's imperative that you learn to transform what you've envisioned into reality. These were my steps for ensuring that I didn't hinder the law of action with the destructive force of inaction:

1: The Ten Second Countdown.
Just fucking go. You've got 10 seconds to get your ass engaged, and if you don't you'll torpedo your idea, and your dream. Obey the impulse and make it physical. Write it down, stand up, open the laptop, something. Within ten seconds, cause something in the physical world to move, or else. The comfort zone of inaction is strong, but you know it too well and the bag of nothin'

that it's bought you so far. You have to force yourself into action, and there's no way around it. Like jumping into a pool that you know is cold, you know damn well that you could hesitate forever. You could sit on the edge and look at everyone having a good time, or you can go. Putting your tip-toe into the water will not work, you've gotta leap. Give yourself the gift of diving in feet first and setting something in motion. I sat down in front of my computer, and literally said, "I'm giving myself to the count of ten. Before I get there, I'd better be typing," and I did. Literally, before I could even get to the count of five my fingers were moving furiously in a free-write that made little sense, but felt awesome to get on paper. I looked up and had a page done of a book I never thought I would get off the ground. So, don't wait. Take massive action from the beginning with a countdown from ten and watch how far you can go.

2: Rig the future in your favor.

I found out the best way to predict tomorrow was to set it up today. For example, the reason I knew I was going to the gym tomorrow is because the night before, I put my gym shoes and sweats directly on the side of my bed. I knew specifically that I was not going to lose my keys because I hung them on the nail by my door. And guess what; the next morning they were right there. They didn't grow legs and walk off; they stayed put, and that's where I found them. The next morning when my alarm clock rang, I forced myself up in under ten seconds. Lo and behold, there was everything I needed to follow through. It's as if some psychic being set up my morning the night before, and knew exactly how it was going to turn out. Some people call this, "planning." However, setting up the future is a more helpful way to view it. The mindset is empowering because it puts you into the now. When you realize that the future doesn't exist, things get clearer. All we're doing is using this present moment to set up the next present moment, because we experience it all as "now." It's almost like we're rigging the game to go the way we like. All we have to do is physically move things into place to sculpt the outcomes we want, and before we know it, they come to pass.

3: Identify as the person you will become.
Until you identify yourself as the thing you are after, you will continue to spin your wheels. For example, during the process of writing this book I underwent a shift in how I saw myself. I began to identify as an "author," not just not just a guy who was trying to write his first book. Before long, it was a part of conversation. Whenever I was out a social events and cocktail parties, "author" was among the things on the list of my titles. I cannot tell you how significant this is. Authors write tons of books, which means that they do more than start; they finish their projects as well. This was a great reminder to someone who had difficulty completing his ideas. Therefore, it was paramount that I saw myself as the person who does this as a matter of course. Identity is a flexible thing, but its power to shape outcomes is bordering absolute. If you're someone who is 'trying to get in shape,' you may or may not get to the gym. If you change your identity to that of an athlete, working out becomes second nature. You don't even have to remind yourself, because you are an athlete. To call yourself that means you are always pushing your body, which means healthy dieting and the gym are a part of your

life, consistently. Whatever your goal is, begin to identify as the person who already has obtained it. This creates a magnetic draw to your outcome that pulls you to its completion rather than you having to push yourself.

4: Create Positive Peer Pressure.

Humans are social animals, so use that to your advantage. Telling positive people about your passion project is a great way to make sure you follow through with it. Notice I said, "positive people." We all know that there are those dream-killing specialists, those assassins of vision that make it all too clear that they don't believe in you, and you shouldn't either. Don't tell them. However, letting those positive people in on your vision is one of the surest ways to trigger yourself into not just starting, but completing your project. Once you get underway, there will be distractions and pitfalls along the way. Why not use the power of peer pressure to push you through? When I began to write the book you are reading, I told my followers on social media that this book was in process. Before I knew it, folks were calling for a pre-ordered copy. There were hundreds of likes and dozens of comments. Now, either I write the book or lose all credibility. There was no choice but to finish the project, and that's exactly what I did.

5. Make it religious: The Secret to Completion.

Whatever your idea is, consistency is key in its realization. If you want it done in a timely fashion, working on your goal must become a habit. Small disciplines achieved over a period of time make the difference in our destinies. For me, writing and creating are a part of my walk in life. What I create is literally an expression of how well I am processing my journey on Earth. Whether it is poetry, drawing, journalism, exercise, or this book, there is a spiritual element to it all. How could there not be? Is this not life a spiritual journey? Perhaps spirit can be best defined as the energy you most frequently operate in. This energy is cultivated through consistency. At the end of the day, we are the result of our rituals, a.k.a, what we do on a regular basis. This can be said to be our true religion. Your passion project, your dream, must become something that you commit your energy to on a regular basis as if you were a Levite, Monk, or Disciple. This was a hard one for me. Consistency was something that I struggled with for most of my life, even from the days of childhood. I would start, and then stop. Before I knew it, months had gone by and the fiery muses that gave me my vision had long since departed. I was left wondering what could have been, time after time. I even prayed to God for the power of consistency, to make the accomplishment of my goal a religious thing. This created some pretty severe pain inside. Feelings of inadequacy haunted me. My un-manifested ideas started to feel like lost children that I would never see again. So acute was this pain, that by the time I started working on a consistent basis manifesting my ideas, I felt a deep and abiding jubilation. It felt so good to work on my visions, I started to wonder, "Why would I deny myself this feeling? Working on this feels incredible." I was pulled toward my goal, not arduously working toward it. There was not that arduous crawl toward my destination, but a joyful consistent bounding pace. It became spiritual because it literally lifted my spirits to do, and this is exactly what I wish for you

In the end, your vision could or could not happen. As real as it feels to you, there is an equal possibility that it will not come to pass for the rest of us. It may collect dust in the un-manifested dimension, the implicate order, and follow you to your grave. The world and the universe are ultimately indifferent to whether you do it or not. The only thing standing in the way of your ideas becoming is how well you employ the law of action. It is the master key to the world we actually live in. The law of action is self-evident and self-enforcing. It is the dominant law of the physical realm. All other laws are subservient to it, and kneel before its preeminence. Time and space are your sculptor's clay for as long as you have a heartbeat. How will you rig the future for your success? Do you have the guts to force yourself into uncomfortable action? Can you follow through religiously to see the desires of your heart come to be?

There is one final thing I want you consider. That is the fact that more people may be depending on you than you realize. Who knows how many countless people could be influenced by your actions, and touched by your creations? Do you want to be the reason they are robbed of the thing that could redirect the course of their lives? Is that what you want to take with you to the grave? I am guessing the answer is no. Well, either you take action, or action takes you! Since none of us know when the grim reaper will come a knocking, you'd better get off your ass. Make damn sure you make moves to manifest your potential. The one the world is waiting for...could be you!

ABOUT THE AUTHOR

Theo Wilson is a Denver native. He graduated from Florida A&M University with a B.A. in Performing Arts. Theo is a four-time TEDx presenter and hopes these words motivate, touch and inspire greatness in you.

Made in the USA
Monee, IL
11 January 2023